EXPLORING
FAITH
Theology for Life

SERIES EDITORS: Leslie J Francis and Jeff Astley

GOD'S WORLD

Jeff Astley

DARTON·LONGMAN+TODD

TiSec

First published in 2000 by
Darton, Longman and Todd Ltd
1 Spencer Court
140-142 Wandsworth High Street
London SW18 4JJ

ISBN 0-232-52367-3

A catalogue record for this book is available from the British Library.

Designed by Sandie Boccacci
Phototypeset in Minion by Intype London Ltd
Printed and bound in Great Britain by
Page Bros, Norwich, Norfolk

CONTENTS

PREFACE

At the beginning of the third millennium a new mood is sweeping through the Christian Churches. This mood is reflected in a more radical commitment to discipleship among a laity who wish to be theologically informed and fully equipped for Christian ministry in the secular world.

Exploring Faith: theology for life is designed for people who want to take Christian theology seriously. Taken seriously, Christian theology engages the mind, involves the heart, and seeks active expression in the way we live. Those who explore their faith in this way are beginning to shape a theology for life.

Exploring Faith: theology for life is rooted in the individual experience of the world and in the ways through which God is made known in the world. Such experience is related to and interpreted in the light of the Christian tradition. Each volume in the series takes a key aspect of theology, and explores this aspect in dialogue with the readers' own experience. Each volume is written by a scholar who has clear authority in the area of theology discussed and who takes seriously the ways in which busy adults learn.

The volumes are suitable for all those who wish to learn more about the Christian faith and ministry, including those who have already taken Christian basic courses (such as *Alpha* and *Emmaus*) and have been inspired to undertake further study, those preparing to take theology as an undergraduate course, and those already engaged on degree programmes. The volumes have been developed for individuals to work on alone or for groups to study together.

Already groups of Christians are using the *Exploring Faith: theology for life* series throughout the United Kingdom, linked by an exciting initiative pioneered jointly by the Anglican dioceses, the Board of Education of the Church and World Division and the Ministry Division of the Archbishops' Council of the Church of England, the National Society and the Church Colleges. Used in this way each volume can earn credits towards one of the Church Colleges' Certificates and provide access to degree level study. Further information about the Church Colleges' Certificate Programme is provided on page 125.

The Church Colleges' Certificate Programme integrates well with the life-long learning agenda which now plays such a crucial role in educational priorities. Learning Christians can find their way into degree-bearing programmes through this series *Exploring Faith: theology for life* linked with the Church Colleges Certificates.

This series of books originated in materials developed by and for the Aston Training Scheme. Thanks are due to former staff of the Scheme, and in particular to Roger Spiller who conceived of and commissioned the original series, and to Nicola Slee who edited the original materials. In the light of the closure of Aston, this series represents something of the ongoing contribution of the Scheme to the life of the Church.

In preparing a series of this kind, much work is done behind the scenes. Financial and staff support have been generously given by the Ministry Division. Thanks are due to Marilyn Parry for the vision of bringing together the Aston materials and the Anglican Church Colleges of Higher Education. We are also grateful for financial support from the following Church Colleges: Chester College; Christchurch University College, Canterbury; The College of St Mark and St John, Plymouth; St Martin's College, Lancaster; Trinity College Carmarthen; and Whitelands College (Roehampton Institute). Without the industry, patience, perception, commitment and skill of Ruth Ackroyd this series would have remained but a dream.

The series editors wish to express their personal thanks to colleagues who have helped them shape the series identity, especially Diane Drayson, Evelyn Jackson and Katie Worrall, and to the individual authors who have produced high quality text on schedule and so generously accepted firm editorial direction. The editorial work has been supported by the North of England Institute for Christian Education and the Centre for Ministry Studies at the University of Wales, Bangor.

Leslie J Francis
Jeff Astley

INTRODUCTION

This book explores the Christian account of God's relationship to the universe. That is, of course, a very broad topic indeed and I have had to be selective for this introductory text. Nevertheless, we shall range quite widely over the issues involved, investigating in some detail the doctrines of creation, providence, miracle, life after death and 'the last things'; as well as discussing the problems of evil and suffering and of science and religion, and some central aspects of the nature and character of God. We shall also touch on long-running debates within theology over such thorny problems as answers to prayer, the doctrine of the Fall, the scope of God's knowledge and power, the freedom of the will, universalism and the Christian approach to the environment.

The text has been shaped so as to help you to understand the logic and implications of traditional Christian beliefs in these areas; to appreciate the intellectual, moral and spiritual criticisms that have been made of many of these beliefs; and to think through a systematic theology of your own that has intellectual coherence and is rooted in your own insights. Reference will be made throughout to the biblical foundations of doctrine and the writings of key classical and contemporary theologians, and you will find plenty of references, quotations and suggestions for further reading (both introductory and advanced). I have attempted to recognise the breadth of the Christian tradition and to review different viewpoints on contentious issues. On occasions, however, I have been rash enough to indicate the direction in which I think that the argument should go.

The subject area 'God and the world' has given rise to theological concepts and arguments that are more philosophically developed than in some other areas of Christian belief. The text is designed to encourage you to analyse this abstract material with the assistance of many concrete illustrative metaphors and analogies. These serve not only as educational aids but also as a constant reminder that if we are to use human language about God (and what is the alternative?), we shall have to speak in similes, parables, stories and figures of speech.

This is not simply a textbook in philosophical theology. The intellectual discussions concerning the credibility and justification of Christian beliefs are accompanied wherever appropriate by an exploration of more existential and spiritual concerns. That is entirely appropriate in a volume that forms part of an adult Christian education series. At the heart of the enterprise of Christian learning there must be a conversation between the learner's own experience, perceptions and emphases and the diverse riches of the traditions of Christian texts, histories, arguments and lives. It is in this conversational dialogue that Christian truth is heard and responded to, and revised and renewed. Every generation needs to engage in this activity for itself, in order to forge, test and strengthen its own theology.

Although *God's World* is intended primarily for adult Christian learners, it should also prove useful for introductory courses in Christian theology or philosophy of religion in sixth forms, colleges and universities. Much of the material in this book has its origins in courses that I have taught in these different contexts.

Quotations from the Bible are from the *New Revised Standard Version* (NRSV) or *Good News Bible* (GNB), as indicated.

1. GOD AND THE UNIVERSE

Introduction

It is often said that theology must begin with God. This is undeniable. God's existence and nature, revelation and action are the subject-matter of theology. But in another sense theology should begin with *us*. It employs our language and logic (or else we could not understand it), and it must be rooted in our experiences, beliefs and activity (otherwise we would reject it as irrelevant to our lives). To use the popular metaphors, theology must be 'earthed' and it must 'keep one foot on the ground' at least.

It is appropriate, therefore, to begin our study of theology where we are, and particularly with 'the world' – not just our own or other people's world of human experience but also the wider world of which our world is an integral part.

The world is understood here *very* widely. We are not concerned simply with the planet earth but with what is spoken of as the 'universe' ('all existing things' – other than God), the 'cosmos' (the universe as an ordered whole) or 'Nature' (the physical world and its interactions, including the biological world of living things).

Reflecting on experience
What comes into your mind when you think of your place in, and relationship with, the 'universe' or 'Nature'?

Some people feel a close kinship to Nature – in their garden or out on the hills, or even when staring up into the Milky Way on a clear night. 'You are a child of the universe no less than the trees and the stars', the *Desiderata* poster declares. 'You have a right to be here.'

The world, then, is a home. But not everyone feels like this, not all the time anyway. We can also be struck by the emptiness, indeed loneliness, of the universe; and the Bible sometimes uses our experience of the awesome fearfulness of Nature to put us in our place (cf. Psalm 8:3–4; Isaiah 40:18–26).

And yet God is affirmed in the Christian creeds as 'the maker of heaven and earth', 'the maker of all things'. So this universe has been made: intended and planned, crafted and developed.

It is *God's world*.

What on earth is creation?

> **EXERCISE**
> Try to sum up for yourself what you think the religious doctrine of creation is about, and what sort of a belief or theory it is.

You might have looked up the word 'creation' in a dictionary. The *Concise Oxford English Dictionary* defines the verb 'create' as 'bring into existence', 'give rise to', 'make by one's actions'. Note two things about this definition. First, the verb is used of the actions of human beings; but second, as a stab at a *theological* notion of creation, the definition is only half adequate. A more accurate explanation of the term as it is applied to God would express the beliefs (a) that the universe was once brought into being by God out of nothing, and (b) that it was, is, and always will be absolutely dependent on God for its existence. We shall explore this definition further in Chapter 2.

What sort of a belief is it? Most theologians would claim that the doctrine of creation is not a scientific theory. It is not a part of science, as is the 'Big Bang' theory which claims that the universe started its life with the explosion of a massive concentration of all its matter, and as a result is still expanding fifteen thousand million years later. This account is a part of physics, the science of matter and energy and space and time; it is not part of theology. Scientific 'cosmology' (or 'cosmogony') often uses the word 'creation' of the origin of things but it does not go back 'behind' the matter or energy in the universe to ask where it comes from or why its expansion started; nor does it refer anywhere to God. Science, in order to be science, can say nothing about the activity of a being that forms no part of the universe.

The theological doctrine of creation performs a different task from any of science's theories about the origins of things. It offers us a personal-purposive, rather than a scientific-causal, explanation of the universe. It tells us about the purpose (the 'why') of the world, not about what goes on within it (the 'how') (see Chapter 5).

Believing and philosophising

In fact creation is both a *metaphysical* and a *religious* view. A 'metaphysical' account is one that provides an all-embracing interpretation of reality and goes beyond the 'empirical' realm (by which we mean the world that can be perceived by our senses, or inferred from what they show us). Theologians rightly argue, however, that the religious and personal dimension of the doctrine is more fundamental. Creation is essentially a confession of *our* absolute dependence on God. This view is expressed in Martin Luther's *Sermons on the Catechism* of 1528: 'The creation . . . means that I believe that God has given to me body, life, reason, and all that I possess. These things I have not of myself, that I may not become proud' (Dillenberger, 1961, p. 209).

This personal confession comes first. Some 'existentialist' thinkers have refused to go beyond it, rejecting the doctrine's broader, metaphysical implications. They understand creation *solely* in religious terms or in terms of human existence, translating it into the claim that human beings receive their authentic existence as a gift from outside themselves. Rudolf Bultmann writes: 'The affirmation that God is creator cannot be a theoretical statement about God as *creator mundi* [= 'creator of the world'] in a general sense. The affirmation can only be a personal confession that I understand myself to be a creature which owes its existence to God' (Bultmann, 1960, p. 69).

Creating and redeeming

Now, it is true that the history and logic of the doctrine of creation suggest that it first arose as an extension of, and as a presupposition for, the religious experience of salvation and the universal human search for meaning in life. The creation stories in Genesis 1 and 2 (and we must note at once that there are *two* stories there, written at different times and expressing different theologies) really serve as a preface to the salvation history that follows. Karl Barth argues: 'Creation is one long preparation ... for what God will intend and do with it in the history of the covenant. Its nature is simply its equipment for grace' (Barth, 1958, p. 231).

> The Hebrew people came to a belief in creation neither through a philosophical analysis of the origin of things, nor through a search for a first Cause. On the contrary, they found God as he acted in history and it was because they were convinced that God is the Lord of all nations that they were led to see that he is the Creator. (Hordern, 1969a, p. 78)

Hence Claus Westermann can write that in the Old Testament the creation of the world 'is not an object of belief, but a presupposition of thou t' (Westermann, 1971, p. 114).

EXERCISE
📖 **Read Isaiah 42:5–6; 43:1; 54:5.**

What is the relationship between redemption (liberation, salvation) and creation in these passages?

Creation and redemption both derive from God. They represent the two fundamental doctrines of Christian theology and should not be split apart. Unfortunately, attempts have been made from time to time to do just that. Gnosticism, one of the earliest challenges to Christian belief, held that the God who created the world was not the same God who redeemed men and women from the world. This view was definitively rejected as heresy (false belief) by the Church, which insisted that the salvation of individuals and nations is a part of the history of the world that God creates. For Paul, the natural world itself yearns for the final liberation of the children of God (Romans 8:22–23). One scholar writes: 'creation means that the evil powers are defeated, and that the order of the world is established for ever ... Creation, therefore, is also a redemptive act' (Ringgren, 1963, p. 63).

Christian theology at its most consistent has insisted that the metaphysical implications of the doctrine of creation have been validly drawn. The God who creates, sustains and redeems me, and the whole people of God, is also active beneath every atom of matter and erg of energy throughout the whole universe. The basic difficulty with the existentialist account is that our human existence is an *in-the-world* existence. So the religious view inevitably leads us to make all-embracing, metaphysical claims. God's action must be a cosmic event.

Picturing God and the world

We need to say something now about the status of the universe, as it is expressed in the doctrine of creation. What is the 'relative importance' of the world in theology? What, in particular, is its relationship to God? To answer these questions we may need to begin again further back, and introduce a few technical words.

I have illustrated some of the terms that theology uses for talking about God and the world in the diagram on p. 6. The arrow represents the universe, and the shaded circle represents God.

Naturalism is the view that only the world of Nature exists. It denies that there is any supernatural being or activity. This is the belief held by most people who call themselves atheists. *Pantheism* is a form of naturalism. It still uses God-language, but applies that language simply and solely to the world. For pantheists, *God = the world*. (The word 'pantheism' translates as 'everything-is-God-ism'.) For this point of view, God is another (more religious) name for the universe; but God does not exist as separate from, or more than, the universe. There is, obviously, no place for any belief in creation on this account of things. The position was held by the seventeenth-century philosopher Spinoza, who argued that the universe consisted of only one substance ('God, or Nature').

Transcendent theism, more usually written just as *theism*, is the traditional option in the Jewish, Christian, Muslim and Sikh faiths, as well as among some Hindus and Buddhists. For the theist, God and the world are radically different realities that are connected by a one-way relationship of dependence. The theist claims that the universe depends on God for its continued existence. Most theists add that God is independent of the universe: if the world could somehow be taken away this would not threaten God's existence nor reduce God's being, because the universe is no part of God. These implications of theism have been captured in a couple of equations (cf. Temple, 1953, p. 435):

The World – God = 0 (the universe without God would be reduced to nothing).
However, *God – the World = God* (God would remain if the universe ceased to exist).

Naturalism
(The world alone exists)

Pantheism
*(God is
world shaped)*

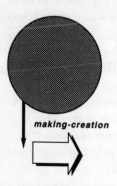

making-creation

Deism
*(The world is made
then left alone by God)*

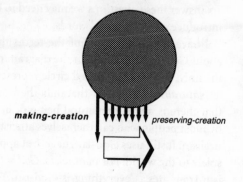

making-creation   *preserving-creation*

Theism
*(The world is both made
and sustained by God)*

or

Panentheism
*(The world is in God: sustained, and probably made, by God;
it may be regarded as a part of God)*
Cf. Peacocke, 1996, pp. 24–27

For theism, God both created the world and continues to keep it in existence, but usually it is only God's *activity* that 'connects' with, 'is present to' or 'penetrates' the world. Creation is, as it were, 'action at a distance'.

A God of parts?

Panentheism, by contrast, is a version of theism that holds that in some sense or other the world is a part of God, but that God is more than just the world. ('Panentheism' translates as 'everything-is-*in*-God-ism'.) On this view, all created things exist 'in God' and God is in all things. Paul spoke of God as one in whom 'we live and move and have our being' (Acts 17:28 NRSV), and Augustine pictured the creation as a huge sponge, existing within, penetrated by and 'filled through and through with the water of [the] boundless sea' that represents the infinite God (Augustine, 1961, p. 138). As we shall see in Chapter 8, in 'process theology' the being of God changes along with the world, to an extent that God is said not only to 'penetrate' but also to 'encompass' and 'include' the world. All events exist 'in God', although God is still described as transcending ('going beyond') the world and the changing part of his own being.

For some, the best way of picturing the relationship is to regard the universe as God's cosmic *body*, and to describe God as including and interacting with the events of the world as a human self or mind interacts with the human brain. A N Whitehead uses a different image from another great Christian doctrine to illuminate the relationship: 'The world lives by its incarnation of God in itself' (Whitehead, 1926, p. 156). On all such views, God is 'world-inclusive, incorporating the world into the divine self' (Suchocki, 1992, p. 341). Hence, the life of the world is the life of God: 'God does not exist except in and through [the] processes' unfolding in the universe; but God is the creative agent who acts in, and therefore is more than, these processes (Tracy, 1984, p. 112).

In panentheism, the relationship of God to the world is one of *interdependence*; it is a two-way, interactive relationship. The universe owes its creation (probably) and its preservation (certainly) to God; but because it is a part of God, and because God loves it, God is open to and affected by everything that happens in the world. This effect is not just on how God functions (feels, cares, thinks, acts); the world also affects how God *is*. To revise our earlier equation, for panentheism:

> God – the World = a reduced God (something less than God; the divine self reduced, although still existing).

But there are dangers here. Pause for a moment, and reflect what they might be.

The idea that the world is a 'part' of God is insisted on by some (take for example Hartshorne, 1953, p. 511: 'what is in the parts is in the whole'; and Jantzen, 1984, p. 149: 'all reality is from God and ultimately not separable from him'). But it is strenuously denied by others, on the grounds that as God is ultimately different from whatever he creates, the world is not 'of the same stuff or "substance" as God himself' (Peacocke, 1993, p. 371). Put more succinctly, 'the world is "in" God, but not "of" God' (Peacocke, 1996, p. 13). Augustine, too, refused to accept any identification of God and the world that implied that 'anything that anyone treads underfoot would be a part of God' (Augustine, 1972, p. 152). I have tried to picture both positions in the diagrams for panentheism.

Baby creation

Nevertheless, according to Arthur Peacocke it might still be proper to think of the universe as created *within* God, as a woman creates – and is interrelated with – her baby within her own body. This certainly offers us a more interdependent and intimate understanding of the creation and preservation of the universe than some other analogies. At least until many months into a pregnancy, the child cannot live outside the mother's womb; similarly, the dependent universe separated from God would cease to exist. And, despite Peacocke's comments above, the mother who loses her baby might claim to have in some sense lost 'a part of herself', organically as well as psychologically.

> The concept of God as Creator has, in the past, been too much dominated by a stress on the externality of God's creative acts – he is regarded as creating something external to himself, just as the male fertilizes the womb from outside. But mammalian females, at least, create within themselves and the growing embryo resides within the female body and this is a proper corrective to the masculine picture – it is an analogy of God creating the world within herself, we would have to say. . . . God creates a world that is in principle and in origin, other than him/herself but creates it, the world, within him/herself. (Peacocke, 1979, p. 142)

> **EXERCISE**
> Reflect on the above quotation, asking yourself how adequate you find this image of the relationship between God and the world, both theologically *and devotionally*.
>
> Is 'procreation' a proper metaphor for creation?
>
> How does our use of the masculine pronoun for God, and the biblical metaphor of 'father', affect our understanding of the relationship between God and the world?

Clocks and creation

The diagram printed above should also help us to differentiate an orthodox (= 'right believing') doctrine of creation from the heresy, or heterodox ('other believing') position, of *deism*. Deism developed in England and France in the seventeenth and eighteenth centuries, but the theology it presents had been repudiated earlier by John Calvin as 'cold and lifeless' (1559, 1, 16, 1). It affirms the existence of a remote God who brought the world into existence, but who neither preserves it nor continues to care for it through any further activity of providence, grace, revelation or miracle. The world, the deists argued, is like a great mechanical clock. Once made, it will run on in the absence of its maker. God produced all the matter and energy of the universe, and the laws of their interaction, but then had nothing further to do with it.

Such a view is in sharp contrast with *theism's* emphasis on God's activity of creative preservation, and the claims of most Christians about God's providential and intervening care and saving help directed towards the creation. For theism, the analogy is not with a clockwork clock but with a mains electric clock that needs continuing contact with its source of power in order to operate. (The analogy is as inadequate as that of the pregnant mother, however, for God keeps the universe in existence and not just functioning.)

Panentheism stays close to theism in stressing this continuing preserving relationship between God and the universe, although some process thinkers believe that the universe is everlasting and therefore reject an originating act of creation.

Is the world real?

There has been tension down the centuries between two different tendencies in Christian theology. One stresses the absolute dependence of all things on God, while the other envisages the creation as having some measure of independence over against its creator. Where the pull towards independence is the stronger influence there is a real danger of ending up in deism, with a completely autonomous universe that is as independent of its creator as a clock is of its maker. But if we seek to avoid deism by allowing ourselves to be pulled too far in the opposite direction, the end result may be a view of Nature as having no independence whatever. A middle way between these two extremes is sometimes expressed in terms of the 'independent causality' of Nature.

On the view of absolute dependence, all events in the universe are wholly determined by God's activity, rather than by anything within Nature itself. The most extreme version of this is sometimes called 'voluntarism', and is rejected by most theologians. For voluntarism, God effects changes in Nature in a way similar to a computer program producing changes on a computer screen. When the computer game is running, the laser gun seems to be blasting the aliens out of the sky. But there is no real *causal connection* between the image of the gun on the screen and the image of the zapped alien. The alien explodes after the gun fires only because the program produces the images in that order.

EXERCISE
Is the world like a computer-generated image? What are the implications of this model of Nature?

You might argue that this 'virtual' world of Nature is a bit of a sham, like the computer game. Nothing is caused by anything else within this world; it is all just God's (regular and orderly) activity. For the eighteenth-century theologian Jonathan Edwards, nothing persists for more than a moment in time, so the existence of any created thing is 'wholly the effect of God's immediate power, in that moment, without any dependence on prior existence, as much as the first creation out of nothing' (Edwards, 1970, p. 402).

But theology has usually favoured an account that gives Nature more reality, some true causality and a bit of 'distance' from God. An alternative image that captures this relationship better is the picture of God as a snooker table! The preserving activity of God 'underlies' Nature, represented here by the balls ricocheting off one another according to physical laws that belong to the balls themselves. God is to be found 'below' Nature, sustaining and upholding the rolls and collisions of the balls; keeping the game 'up and running' according to its own order and rules.

EXERCISE
Is this image of a snooker table any better? What are the implications of this picture of creation?

Of course snooker tables don't *create* snooker balls or the laws of their interaction, so the analogy is inadequate on that count. And the table doesn't get up and use a cue to set the balls rolling either. But as an image of non-interfering preservation of an intrinsic order and causality within Nature, perhaps it isn't too bad.

However, both pictures are excessively impersonal and mechanical. In the next chapter we must try to remedy that.

Further reading

Introductory
Barth, K (1966), *Dogmatics in Outline*, ET London, SCM, chapter 9.
Thomas, O C (1983), *Introduction to Theology*, Wilton, Connecticut, Morehouse, chapter 6.
Westermann, C (1974), *Creation*, ET London, SPCK, chapter 5.
Young, N (1976), *Creator, Creation and Faith*, London, Collins, chapter 7.

Advanced
Gilkey, L (1959), *Maker of Heaven and Earth*, New York, Doubleday.
Jantzen, G M (1984), *God's World, God's Body*, London, Darton, Longman and Todd.
Peacocke, A (1996), *God and Science: a quest for Christian credibility*, London, SCM, chapter 1.
Tracy, T F (1984), *God, Action, and Embodiment*, Grand Rapids, Michigan, Eerdmans.
Woods, G F (1958), *Theological Explanation*, Welwyn, Nisbet, chapter XV.

2. THE MEANING OF CREATION

Introduction

In this chapter we shall consider the doctrine of creation in more depth and detail. Like any concept it has a 'logic', in the sense that it serves as shorthand for a particular set of implications (about God, the world, Nature, the meaning of life, etc.) and a particular way of dealing with and relating to other concepts (especially those of 'God' and 'the world').

Before we unpack and discuss the doctrine further, however, it may be worthwhile to look back at our attempts to define the word 'creation' in the last chapter. In particular, note again that the word is applied in the dictionary to the activities of human beings as well as those of God. It would be useful to explore now how we use the language of creation when speaking of ourselves and one another.

Reflecting on experience
Think about aspects of your own life and work that you or others might describe as 'creative'. Consider first your present range of activities, and then review your past life looking for other times and situations of particular creativity. What is *creative* about you?

We only have human language to portray God. But in many ways God's creative work is unique, *sui generis* ('of its own kind'). We can only understand it by employing analogies and metaphors that draw on the everyday examples and occasions of human creativity. In this way our sweat and skill and care can be used, however inadequately, to model the nature and character of God.

Modelling creation

Theology uses figurative language, in the shape of metaphors and models (a 'model' is a metaphor that is employed in a sustained and systematic way). They give us some insight into the nature of the mysterious, transcendent God, but they cannot be applied literally. (Some theologians distinguish such metaphorical language from the use of analogy in speaking of God. An analogy is a comparison or simile, a likeness-with-difference, which may be said to apply literally to God, as when we say that God is 'living' or 'acts'. Others place both analogy and metaphor into the category of figurative speech.)

Sub-personal models
One historically popular account of creation interprets it on the model of rays of light emanating from the sun. One thing in favour of this model is that the light is *dependent* on the sun; but unfortunately the picture is often developed so as to suggest that the world is made of the same substance as God, or that it is only an 'appearance' of God. This impersonal model also implies that God cannot help producing the creation, whereas theology usually insists that the universe is the product of God's intentional will.

Personal models
The preferred way of speaking of the creator is through a range of personal models:
- God as gardener – designing, nurturing, tending (and selectively destroying?) an independent creation which has its own nature;
- God as lord or king – one who rules over a dependent world through the exercise of sovereign power;
- God as architect or designer – creating the great plan and adapting different elements to fit into it;
- God as fabricator (weaver, sculptor, potter, painter) – one who comes out of the drawing office and actually fashions a work of art or craft;
- God as speaker, actor, musician or dancer. Unlike the human models we have explored so far, the creations of these people only exist *as they are created*. Such continuing creations are often particularly vivid and personal expressions of their creators. Creation is thought of here not so much as work, but rather as the 'play' of God: 'a kind of free artistic expression [of] ... God's good pleasure' (Migliore, 1991, p. 93; cf. Moltmann, 1985, pp. 310–312);

- God as novelist, dramatist, poet, composer or choreographer. In some cases this involves the creation of a personal, 'independent' character with a nature that even its creator must respect. (So Agatha Christie cannot make Miss Marple behave like Hercule Poirot, for that would be 'out of character'.) Other artistic creations can also acquire a 'life of their own', a semi-autonomous existence dependent on their 'recreation' by performers;
- Creation as 'suicide-in-reverse'. My suicide would be the complete destruction of my 'whole world'; God's creation is the opposite;
- The world interpreted as a body, with God as its 'soul' or 'mind'. Traditionally, God is thought of as a 'discarnate' (bodyless) Spirit who could exist without any world. Some, however, understand God as an essentially embodied person, sometimes arguing that God could not exist without *some* world. Several implications flow from this view: for example that God may need the world for his self-expression and 'full' life, and that all events are God's 'basic actions' performed directly as a person raises her arm;
- *Parent-models* – in Chapter 1 we explored the language of generation or procreation, with God pictured as a parent loving a child into existence. But children are not just for conception and pregnancy! Parents also serve as models for God in their role as nurturers of their children's (relatively) independent personhood, through their self-giving love.

EXERCISE
📖 **Read Hosea 11:1–9.**

In the Bible parental language is usually used about God with reference to this sort of love and care, rather than procreation. Is parenting a good model for creation? What are its strengths and weaknesses compared with the other models?

You might have reasoned that the point of parenthood is to create offspring who no longer need their parents, whereas the universe will always be dependent on God. But there are limitations in all these models. God alone can bring things into existence out of nothing, humans can 'create' only by manipulating stuff that already exists. And most models do not even hint at God's activity of keeping things in existence.

Beginnings and continuings

The definition given in Chapter 1 recognises two elements in the doctrine of creation:

- God's creating of the universe out of nothing, at the beginning of time; and
- God's continuing act of keeping the universe in being.

Thus God is the cause not only of the coming-into-being, but also of the continuing-in-being of the world. This second element is sometimes referred to as *continuing (or continuous) creation*.

Many argue that God's activity in creating and sustaining the world is essentially the same, and that God is no more directly involved in the origin of things than in their continuing existence. Others, however, distinguish the acts of originating and conserving on the grounds that conservation is directed to something that already exists.

Continuous creation is best thought of as 'the incessant act by which [God] preserves the world in existence' (Mascall, 1956, p. 132), not as a series of separate new acts of bringing-into-existence (despite the diagram in Chapter 1). Certainly, we should not think of the world continually passing out of existence and coming back into existence. If God exists 'outside time', continuous creation is a timeless act from God's standpoint.

EXERCISE
Look up the word 'depend' in a dictionary. What does it mean to say that the world depends on God?

The original meaning of the word 'depend' is 'to hang down'. An appropriate picture here would be a pendant light supported by a wire from the ceiling, or a chandelier held in place by a nut and bolt. Cut the wire or unscrew the bolt and the result does not bear thinking about. Sometimes the analogy is inverted, and God is said to support the universe from below: 'He's got the whole world in his hands'; 'his eternal arms are your support' (Deuteronomy 33:27 GNB).

So God continues to be responsible for the existence of all things, and they continue to be dependent on their creator. It is this element of preservation within the doctrine of creation that allows theologians to sit light to controversies about the beginning of creation. Even if the world were everlasting, and therefore had no beginning, it would still be a 'created' world because its existence is now dependent on God's activity.

> It is not of direct importance to Religion to assert a date for the act of Creation, or even to assert that it is an act having any date at all; it may be a never-beginning and never-ending activity. But it is of vital importance to Religion to assert that the existence of the world is due to the Will of God. This is the essential notion of Creation. (Temple, 1953, p. 37)

But there is a sense in which believers also speak of the world's *independence* (look back at the models for creation earlier in this chapter). So it is said that God 'has created something Other than Himself, "over against" Himself . . . In so doing He limits Himself . . . by the fact that the world over against Himself is a real existence' (Brunner, 1952, pp. 19–20).

The nature of Nature

As we saw in the last chapter, this act of creation-preservation must be understood in a way that allows the universe's own natural order to be a reality, rather than a sham.

EXERCISE

Look again at the computer game and snooker table analogies in Chapter 1. Consider what the real differences are between these two situations:

1. one in which God *continually* and regularly creates things and events in the world anew, so that everything is a direct act of God ('voluntarism'); and
2. one in which God first creates a semi-autonomous world, and then allows it to run on according to its God-given nature by *continuously* keeping it in being.

In fact there would be no *observable* difference between the two situations, provided that God's creative activity in case 1 is regular and predictable. In this case, the 'laws of Nature' would just be the laws of God's activity, describing how God usually does things in the world; they would not be the causal laws of an autonomous Nature. Science could still take place, but it would merely be the discovery of the order in God's mind (the 'program') rather than the order in God's world.

But although we could not tell the difference between cases 1 and 2, there *is* a real difference between them. In case 1 all events in the universe are direct acts of God, so that (for example) God directly causes heavy objects to fall to the ground when they are no longer supported. There is no independent causality in this universe. In case 2, however, such events are only *indirectly* caused by a God who directly creates and sustains all things but has given them causal powers of their own.

In case 2, then, God is the primary, general, universal and uniform cause of everything. But although he is in this way *necessary* for things to happen, God's activity is not *sufficient* on its own to produce the effects that Nature produces. Those effects have in a sense been *mediated* through the causal pathways of the world. As Austin Farrer puts it, 'God not only makes the world, he makes it make itself' (Farrer, 1967, p. 51).

Every event in the world can therefore be analysed into two co-existing actions:
• the genuinely independent causal activity of the world (sometimes called 'secondary causation'); and
• God's primary causation, which is the 'uniform enabling of the secondary causes' power to act' (Wiles, 1986, p. 34).

But we must not think that God creates the laws of Nature separately, and then creates objects that obey those laws. He creates things (or events) of such a nature that they behave in certain regular and predictable ways, interacting with other things and causing other events. This is the sense in which God is responsible for the laws of science.

Both-and creation

In case 2 above, God works through the secondary causes in Nature in the way that a human being uses tools. When we describe the human situation, we happily speak of *both* the woodworker *and* the saw as cutting the wood.

EXERCISE

How adequate is this *both-and* language in speaking of the causality of God and the world? Does it allow the world enough independence?

We often still talk in this both-and way, even when the secondary agent has a great deal of independence, insisting that both the stonemasons and the bishop built the tower, and describing an improvised drama as 'both the author's and the actors" (Wiles, 1986, p. 38).

The place of nothing

According to traditional theology, God did not create the world out of anything. God did not simply shape or change something 'pre-existing', something that already existed independent of God's will (whether 'matter', 'chaos' or 'energy'). Rather, creation is *ex nihilo* ('out of nothing'). Hence God is responsible for the raw materials of creation as well as the final product. Any imperfections in creation are not to be excused as the consequence of working with flawed or intractable material. Naturally, that is a perfectly proper excuse for *us* to use. 'Don't blame the teacher,' we quip, 'blame the students.' 'The plumber did his best, it's these shoddy ballcocks.' But God has no such excuse (see Chapter 6). If the *ex nihilo* doctrine were denied, however, natural evil *could* be traced back to the materials on which the creator worked: 'the raw matter continuously resists his will and seeks to descend once more into chaos' (Vardy, 1992, p. 122).

The conviction that creation is out of nothing first appears explicitly in the Apocrypha to the Old Testament – in 2 Maccabees 7:28, a book written between 100 BC and AD 70. It is sometimes argued that the account of creation in Genesis 1 reveals an earlier view of God creating out of *something*. Thus in 1:2 God seems to be making order out of a chaos that is 'without form and void'. However, most Jewish and Christian scholars claim that, although the Genesis story is mainly concerned with the ordering of chaos, 'it would be false to say . . . that the idea of the *creatio ex nihilo* was not present at all' (von Rad, 1972, p. 51; cf. 1975, pp. 143–144; Eichrodt, 1967, pp. 101–106; Jacobs, 1973, pp. 94–97). That idea is implied in the New Testament (see Romans 4:17; Hebrews 11:3) and comes to full expression with the second-century Christian writer Irenaeus. God is greater than us, he argues, in that God himself 'summoned into existence the material of his creation where before it had not been' (quoted in Norris, 1966, p. 73).

The notion of creation out of nothing is usually applied to the origination of things ('making-creation') but it also has implications for 'preserving-creation'. It expresses the belief that the universe now 'depends on a divine thread of preservation above the abyss of nothingness; at any moment God can let it fall into nothingness' (Brunner, 1952, p. 34). So the world came from nothing and would *return* to nothing, except for God's sustaining activity. At the heart of the doctrine of creation lies the insight that 'if the divine action should cease, all things would drop into nothing instantly' (Aquinas, in Clark, 1972, p. 131).

What else?

If God creates out of nothing, does that mean that there is nothing at all that exists independently of God? He creates all matter and energy and the laws of their interaction (the particular natures and potentialities of things). But does God also create the laws of logic, or are these true of all possible universes? (Logic is a function of human thinking and human language, of course, which are parts of God's creation.) And does God create moral values and moral 'laws', or are they also independent of God's will (see Chapter 6)?

Is time created? Presumably the answer is 'yes', as the universe is a set of things and events related spatially and temporally. According to Augustine, the world was not created 'in time':

> An event in time happens after one time and before another, after the past and before the future. But at the time of creation there could have been no past, because there was nothing created to provide the change and movement which is the condition of time.
>
> The world was in fact made *with* time, if at the time of its creation change and motion came into existence. (1972, p. 436)

But many theologians reject the idea that God is outside all time (see Pike, 1970; Swinburne, 1977b, chapter 12; 1994, pp. 137–144; cf. Gale, 1991, chapters 2 and 3). For them, God is 'eternal' in the sense that God is everlasting rather than timeless, and all time is not created.

Creative implications

> **EXERCISE**
> Now that we have explored the doctrine of creation in some detail, try to jot down a list of its implications for our thinking about God and the world (including us).

You may have noted the following theological and ethical consequences of creation.

- The world is a unity, since God is one.
- The doctrine of creation constitutes a denial of any ultimate dualism (belief in two primary forces). The universe is not another self-sufficient, eternal reality; God alone is sovereign.
- It also implies a rejection of naturalism, pantheism and the view that the world is illusory (see Chapter 1).
- The doctrine opposes the prejudice that the material world is evil, in contrast with such philosophies as Platonism, Gnosticism and Manicheism. It is a good God who is responsible for the existence of matter, and 'God saw everything that he had made, and indeed, it was very good' (Genesis 1:31 NRSV).
- Because 'what takes shape in it is the goodness of God' (Barth, 1958, p. 330), the processes of the universe are also 'reliable and trust-worthy', so that it is 'a home for humans and other forms of life, rather than an uncaring or even hostile environment' (Hefner, 1984, p. 271).
- Clearly the doctrine implies that the existence of the world is dependent on God's will. For Aquinas, 'the world exists just so long as God wills it to, since its existence depends on his will as on its cause' (*Summa Theologiae*, 1a, 46, 1; Vol. 8, 1967, pp. 69–71). Since God chooses to bring it into existence, creation is purposeful and intentional; it has 'meaning'.
- Many claim that creation has moral consequences. They describe it as 'benefit' (Karl Barth) and gift, and argue that human beings must therefore respond to it in gratitude. Yet the world remains God's world: humans only hold it in trust for God. The doctrine is often taken to imply an ecological ethic that claims that we have a duty to care for the world (see Chapter 8).
- It may also be said to imply a sacramental view of Nature, in which the created realm is seen as an environment of God's revelation.

Matter exists 'to be the vehicle of spirit and the sphere of spirit's self-realisation in and through the activity of controlling it' (Temple, 1953, p. 493).

- Who is the world for? Is it just 'for us' – for the sake of human beings; or is it created for other life forms, or 'for itself', or 'for God's sake'? Jürgen Moltmann reminds us that the creation narrative in Genesis 1 does not end with the making of human beings, but in God's sabbath rest and celebration on 'the seventh day'. The sabbath is the point of creation, and the God who rests on the sabbath is the 'rejoicing God, the God who delights in his creation, and in his exultation sanctifies it' (Moltmann, 1985, pp. 276–277; cf. pp. 5–7, chapter XI; see also Moltmann, 1989, pp. 80–87).

- On most accounts of creation, God is ontologically distinct (distinct in being) from the world; he is creator, it is created. God is therefore in a class of his own, for there is no more fundamental distinction than that between dependent, finite, created beings, on the one hand, and their independent, infinite creator, on the other. Many theologians follow Kierkegaard in asserting the 'infinite qualitative difference' between God and the world, particularly the world of human beings. God as creator is *transcendent* over (different from, other than) the creation. But as creator God is also necessarily *immanent* – that is intimately involved with it. Although the metaphors of transcendence ('far off', 'beyond') point in the opposite direction to those of immanence ('close to', 'within'), the doctrine of creation holds the two concepts together.

Further reading

Introductory

Barth, K (1966), *Dogmatics in Outline*, ET London, SCM, chapter 8.

Farrer, A (1966), *A Science of God?*, London, Bles, chapter 5.

Kaufman, G D (1978), *Systematic Theology: a historicist perspective*, New York, Scribners, chapter 20.

Macquarrie, J (1966, 1977), *Principles of Christian Theology*, London, SCM, chapter X.

Migliore, D L (1991), *Faith Seeking Understanding: an introduction to Christian theology*, Grand Rapids, Michigan, Eerdmans, chapter 5.

Quick, O C (1963), *Doctrines of the Creed: their basis in Scripture and their meaning today*, London, Collins, chapter V.

Sayers, D L (1941), *The Mind of the Maker*, London, Methuen.

Vardy, P (1990), *The Puzzle of God*, London, Collins, chapter 14.

Vanstone, W H (1977), *Love's Endeavour, Love's Expense: the response of being to the love of God*, London, Darton, Longman and Todd, chapter 2.

Advanced

Brunner, E (1952), *The Christian Doctrine of Creation and Redemption*, ET London, Lutterworth.

Mascall, E L (1956), *Christian Theology and Natural Science: some questions on their relations*, London, Longmans, Green, chapter 4.

Moltmann, J (1985), *God in Creation: an ecological doctrine of creation*, ET London, SCM.

Owen, H P (1984), *Christian Theism: a study in its basic principles*, Edinburgh, T and T Clark, chapter 1.

Peacocke, A (1993), *Theology for a Scientific Age: being and becoming – natural, divine and human*, London, SCM, pp. 166–177.

Wiles, M (1986), *God's Action in the World*, London, SCM, chapters 2 and 3.

3. ACTS OF GOD: PROVIDENCE

Introduction

In this chapter and the next we shall consider some issues that lie at the heart of Christian spirituality, by reflecting on claims about the further activity of God in the world. Let us start these discussions, therefore, very close to home.

Reflecting on experience

Have you ever thought of any event in your own life, or in the life of someone close to you, as 'providential' or as an 'act of God'? If so, consider what features of that event made you describe it in that way. If not, what *would* make you say of some event that it was an 'act of God'?

The different activities of God

'Act of God' is a phrase that was once widely used by insurance companies to describe the operation of unusual, uncontrollable and destructive natural forces. Religious people tend to use the same words in a more positive, and often in a more everyday, sense when they speak of the ways in which God relates to the world.

Michael Langford distinguishes six different ways in which God may be active (Langford, 1981, pp. 5–24). The first two are contained in a broad understanding of the doctrine of creation, as we saw in Chapter 2. They are *the creative activity of God* as a past, once-for-all event in which God brought the universe into being, and *God's continuing sustaining activity* that keeps the universe in existence.

The third category is *God's action as final cause*. According to Aristotle, the 'final cause' of something is the goal, end or purpose to which it is directed. For religious believers, God is the final cause of the world because God creates a universe that is endowed with a purpose. Creation thus has a 'direction' and an 'end'. As Augustine famously put it, writing of the human creation at the beginning of his *Confessions*: 'You made us for yourself and our hearts find no peace until they rest in you' (Augustine, 1961, p. 21). That purpose is expressed and realised in God's action in creation and preservation, but only in a partial and general way. In this chapter and the next we shall consider some more manifest, particular and direct expressions of God's plan. It is important to remind ourselves at the start, however, that God is already purposefully active in the everyday, ordinary and routine events of the world of Nature, as well as in more particular and unusual situations.

God's purpose of care for us is more clearly revealed in the last three of Langford's categories of God's activity: *general providence, special providence* and *miracle*. We shall explore each of these doctrines in turn.

EXERCISE
📖 **Read Genesis 50:20–21; Psalm 33:13–22; Isaiah 40:10–11; Matthew 5:43–45 and 6:25–34.**

These texts reflect various aspects of God's activity and several ways of thinking about it. While recognising that they come from different parts of the Bible, and were written in very different contexts for distinct purposes and audiences, what *theological* similarities and differences do you notice between these accounts?

There is a lot of rich theology in these texts. They all point to a good, overriding purpose in God's activity. It is a purpose that is expressed in different places (in history and in Nature) and is both *general* and *particular*.

Puzzling over providence

EXERCISE
Before reading any further, consider for a moment the word 'providence'. What other words or ideas does it make you think of? And how would you define it?

You might have come up with some of these words or phrases:

- *good fortune*
- *forethought*
- *'providing for' a spouse or child*
- *vigilance*
- *the opposite of 'improvident'*

- *prudence*
- *foresight*
- *fate, karma, destiny*
- *vision*
- *The Provident Insurance Company (or the like)*

One theologian has defined faith in providence as 'the belief that all things are held in the grasp of an eternal purpose' which is concerned with men and women and their history (Farmer, 1963, p. 95). The doctrine of providence underscores the conviction that the creation is itself redemptive.

The word 'providence' derives from the Latin *providere*, meaning 'to see before' and, by extension, 'to see for' or 'on behalf of'. This suggests the two aspects of the doctrine, which you have probably already noted: *foresight* ('seeing ahead', 'seeing what is going to happen') and *care* ('seeing about', 'providing for').

Providence as foresight

Does God 'see ahead'? The problem here relates to our understanding of God's 'omniscience', which is the power of God to know all that there is to know. Briefly, the difficulty is whether and how God could possibly know all things *in the future*. In particular, how can God know what human beings will do next before they have even decided what they will do themselves?

Theology has offered a number of possible answers. (I omit the philosophically subtle notion of God's 'middle knowledge', which some claim solves the problem at a stroke; see Craig, 1998.)

Answer 1

God knows future events timelessly. On this view, God exists 'outside time' and all human history is experienced by God in one 'timeless moment'. It is as if God were at the summit of a mountain which has a long road winding its way around the base far below. God can see 'at a glance' the beginning, the middle part and the destination of the road; but travellers on the road itself can only see the part of it they are on at the time, different stretches of the road being out of sight of others. On this interpretation, God's knowledge of human acts seems to be compatible with our freedom of decision and action, even though God can see our 'future path'.

But we now have to face the difficulty of understanding how a God who acts in time can be outside of time. And, in any case, can this *spatial* analogy really apply to time?

Answer 2

God knows future events in the same ways that we do. Here God knows the future by prediction and by knowing human intentions (in addition to knowing what he intends to do in the future himself). On this view, however, God may not know some future acts at all. As we shall see in Chapter 7, acts of a free will are in principle unpredictable since they are undetermined and undecided before a certain point in time. And if some events in Nature are not completely determined, as physicists argue, they will also be unpredictable in principle (see Chapter 5). So this interpretation suggests that there is a limit to God's omniscience, and therefore to God's providence.

Answer 3

God knows the future by a special act of precognition. Such 'para-normal' divine knowledge *would* be compatible with our having real free will. However, critics might argue that as future acts do not exist at present they cannot be known in this way, not even by God.

(You will have noticed that in answers 2 and 3 God could exist 'in time', even if it is 'God's time' rather than ours: cf. Psalm 90:4 and Chapter 2 above.)

How clever?

It would seem to be central to the doctrine of providence that God knows the future at least better than we do, but *how much* better? This question applies not just to knowing human acts, but also to God's knowledge of the non-human creation.

Some theologians seem quite content to deny God's omniscience. One writes, 'When a young person dies or a deformed child is born, and people ask, "Did God want this to happen?", the best short answer is "No – he didn't even know it was going to happen"' (Cowburn, 1979, p. 37). This attitude would not have done for Calvin. 'All events whatsoever are governed by the secret counsel of God', he wrote.

'Nothing happens but what he has knowingly and willingly decreed' (1559, 1, 16, 2–3).

Powerful stuff! But what do you think?

EXERCISE

How much do you believe that God knows and can know about the future?

Would God be God for you if, of necessity, he was ignorant of some things that might happen in the world in the future, especially some of your future actions?

Knowing the future and deciding the future

However we understand and limit it, God's foresight should be distinguished from the idea of *predestination* or *foreordination*. These names are given to the divine decree by which a human being's future actions and ultimate salvation are infallibly determined by God.

The difference is this: foreknowledge is passive, while foreordination is active. Foreordination is surely incompatible with any real freedom of the human will. It also seems to make the temporal process of our human history redundant; for what is the point of human life if God has already programmed us to act in certain ways and to achieve a certain destiny?

Some traditions of theology, however, lay great store on God being in control from the outset. For Calvin, God 'directs everything'. But others relish the idea of God creating us as free beings whose actions and destiny are so much our own that we can even surprise our creator. For them, creation implies a large element of *risk-taking*. Creation is not only God's 'letting-be' (Macquarrie, 1966, chapter X), but also a 'letting-go' of control over us that is born of respect for our – and perhaps Nature's – independence. On this account, God's omniscience is self-limited by his choice to create this sort of world. 'God creates a world of life, not knowing precisely what will happen and be done, but knowing rather what he will do whatever his creatures do, and knowing that the eventual outcome will indeed make the whole thing worthwhile' (Hebblethwaite, 1979, p. 448).

It is this eventual outcome that is 'predestined', but only in the sense that God's plan and purposes are steadfast and changeless.

Providence as care

We move on now to the second aspect of providence, God's care. Two types of divine providential care are frequently distinguished, *general* and *special.*

General providence

This term is used to label God's general care for the world through the order of Nature. It has been called God's 'government of the universe through the universal laws that control or influence nature, man, and history' (Langford, 1981, p. 11).

In many ways this idea seems to be just a re-run of the notion of God's continuous creative activity in sustaining the world in being. There is more to it than that, however, and the word 'providence' suggests more of a sense of God's care and concern for his creatures than does the bald notion of 'preservation'. We should think in terms of 'caring preservation' or 'preserving the world for a purpose'. The Protestant *Heidelberg Catechism* of 1563 defines providence in terms of God's power to uphold and rule the creation, 'in such a way that . . . [all things] come to us not by chance but by his fatherly hand' (article 27). Still, the concern remains here at a rather general level. God sends the sun and the rain on the just and on the unjust alike.

The doctrine of general providence nevertheless suggests that there is some *general steering* going on of the course of Nature, evolution and history. An important feature of this is that God's general providential activity in Nature is always capable of a natural explanation – it is 'normal' and predictable (if we exclude the 'indeterminate' subatomic events mentioned earlier). The doctrine has been pictured using the analogy of a boatman steering a boat this way or that along a river, but only within the defined limits of the river banks. To change the analogy, God could be said to be operating here like a pianist playing different musical scales but with each note always falling predictably after the previous one in a uniform sequence. Such behaviour is 'regulated' and 'ordered', 'shaped' and 'directed', 'progressive' and 'developing'.

There is a danger in this idea of general providence. Too much emphasis on the doctrine may lead to a distant and impersonal view of God: God as the principal, head teacher or managing director who guides things at a very general level but does not show any specific 'personal touches' in the classroom or on the shop floor.

EXERCISE

To care for children properly you need to practise *general care* by routinely cooking, washing, cleaning, painting the gutters and paying the mortgage, as well as *particular care* by playing with and feeding your children individually, and taking each of them on holiday. The kids appreciate the particular care more than the general but the good parent has to exercise the more 'distant' sort of care also. This parental 'general providence' is just as much an act of love as the other kind.

How do you respond to this analogy?

Special or particular providence

Here God's purpose is expressed in *specific* events, such as circumstances within the history of Israel or occasions within the natural order of things, which bring aid to individuals or communities. Such events are *ad hoc* acts of God. They are 'special', 'for this particular purpose'. But they remain – like the activity of general providence – within the bounds of Nature. They are therefore capable of a natural (scientific) explanation. They are not unpredictable in principle, although they may be 'unexpected'.

Many 'answers to prayer' fall into this category (but see also Chapter 4). If people pray for rain or healing, some changes may follow in the sky or the sick person's body that are not expected, but are not inexplicable. We could interpret the so-called 'coincidence miracles' in a similar way (as when the doctor drives up just at the moment that you suffer a heart attack).

Particular providence pictures God as more personal or 'involved' in caring for the creation, but this too may be a problem. It may lead to the danger (which it shares with the category of miracle) of sliding into a view of God as one who acts arbitrarily and spasmodically, and is inclined to favouritism. Such a God might care for the just *rather than* the unjust, for the people of Israel but not for those of Syria. But does not God care for everyone?

One of the great themes of the Bible is the idea of Israel as God's elect or chosen one. As it is usually the case that choosing someone implies passing over or neglecting someone else, theology must struggle with the question of how God's election of some fits together with God's caring concern for all.

EXERCISE

  📖 Read Exodus 6:2–9; Psalm 92; Amos 3:2 and 9:7.

How may God's particular choices be reconciled with God's universal love?

This is a very big question. I will suggest a possible response later. But note first that election in the Bible is always election to responsibility, obedience and discipleship; and not for privilege, status or personal power. This helps to explain the reluctance of Moses, Isaiah, Jeremiah, Jonah and others to be chosen at all!

Revisiting 'acts of God'

Theologically, the idea of particular providence is always in danger of collapsing into that of general providence, because a strong view of general providence allows little room for particular providence. Any position that stresses the intimacy of God's presence to the world, through God's continuous creative act and general steering of Nature, will be unwilling to recognise a distinct category of particular providence. Why should it? God is already always as involved with every event 'as one could wish' (Alston, 1985, pp. 213–214). 'All events', wrote C S Lewis, 'are equally providential' (Lewis, 1960, p. 178).

The doctrine of general providence claims that all natural events are already expressions of God's creative care, while at the same time being capable of being understood in terms of scientific causes. Some of these events, we might say, are of *particular significance to us*. They therefore seem 'more providential' than do other events; they are more likely to be experienced by us *as* God's 'caring acts'. But perhaps God is really no more active in these events than elsewhere.

Furthermore, some of God's activities express the divine character more clearly than do others. We should not be puzzled by this, for it is the same with us. Talking to a friend is a more characteristic and personal action than cleaning your teeth. But both are equally your actions. The issue here is whether particular providential events

represent an *additional* category of divine activity – 'deliberate manifes-
tations of his will' (Langford, 1981, p. 74) – as opposed to simply being
particular examples of God's general providential care.

In Chapter 2 we looked at God's preservation of the world and
interpreted this as one incessant act essentially identical to God's bringing of the world into existence. Does this mean, then, that we might
think of God's action as *one uniform and universal action*, directed
towards the world as a whole? Should we think, indeed, of 'the world as
a whole as a single act of God' (Wiles, 1986, p. 29, cf. pp. 107–108)? And
does that mean that we should *not* think of particular occurrences
within the world as different divine actions, the products of particular
new divine initiatives, but as all expressing the same divine activity even
though people will welcome and focus on some of them rather more
than others?

Maurice Wiles argues for this position. What is important, he writes,
is 'the kind of world God has created', rather than 'particular, specifiable
acts of God in history' (p. 62). Other theologians, however, want to
place the emphasis on particular acts of God, especially the incarnation
and resurrection of Christ, often seeing them as *exceptional* types of
activity – in a word as 'interventions'. It is sometimes held that these are
needed because God must react to ('interact' with) the free choices of
human beings in an *ad hoc* way. These events would be God's 'actions'
in a more complete sense than some of the others we have discussed.

While we are engaged in this analysis, let us observe that we usually
speak of a person's action in terms of her *intention*. So, even though
God's agency is necessary for every event to happen, perhaps we should
only identify those events as 'acts of God' that God does not just
cause but also intends – that is, *those that fulfil God's purposes*. Other
events are merely 'allowed' or 'consented to', and God is not directly
responsible for them (Brümmer, 1992, p. 124). Such a distinction might
be useful in discussing the problem of evil (see Chapters 6 and 7).

Redundant activity?

The idea of particular acts of God is frequently said to be redundant, for
God can give us all that we need through his general preserving and
steering of Nature. But is that enough?

Consider another analogy. (It is, I fear, a rather sexist one.) A boy
goes to a party intent on securing a girl – any girl, anyone who will
have him. He circulates and gives all the girls the benefits of his

presence, his acts and his words. This is his 'general care' and his 'general revelation'.

Let us say that one responds. Would any further particular activity on the boy's part now be 'redundant', or even 'unfair' (recall the earlier exercise)? Has he now said and done, to and with them all, all that he wants to say and do? Is it not rather the case that it is only *now*, only when there has been a response, that the real 'revelation' and 'caring' can begin? It was inappropriate before, for there was then no relationship; but now that there has been a particular response, there is room for some particular, additional activity.

And so it is with God. Perhaps there are some things that God can only tell us – for only then will we understand – after we have responded to him. The responders alone will hear these things. Perhaps there are things that God will, or can, only do for us subsequent to our response of faith. We shall receive them only if, and when, we react to him.

God's relation to the world is not necessarily just a matter of God's general activity and our particular response. There is also room for a subsequent stage of God's particular activity in response to *our* response.

The trouble with some accounts of God's dealings with the world is that they expect everything to be as difficult and ambiguous as it can possibly be all the time. But why should it be? If God's purpose is to encourage us freely to come into relationship with him, without first overwhelming us with the divine presence, why should God not make things easier and clearer *subsequent to our initial response*? Such divine activity will not override our freedom, and we cannot accuse God of 'favouritism' for engaging in it, any more than we can raise these charges against the boy at the party.

What do you think?

Further reading

Introductory

Farmer, H H (1963), *The World and God*, London, Collins.

Farrer, A (1967), *Saving Belief: a discussion of essentials*, London, Hodder and Stoughton, pp. 37–58.

Goulder, M and Hick, J (1983), *Why Believe in God?* London, SCM, chapter 4.

Macquarrie, J (1966, 1977), *Principles of Christian Theology*, London, SCM, chapter XI.

Advanced

Brümmer, V (1992), *Speaking of a Personal God*, Cambridge, Cambridge University Press, chapter 5.

Gorringe, T J (1991), *God's Theatre: a theology of providence*, London, SCM.

Hebblethwaite, B and Anderson, E (eds) (1990), *Divine Action*, Edinburgh, T and T Clark.

Kaufman, G D (1972), *God the Problem*, Cambridge, Massachusetts, Harvard University Press, chapter 6.

Langford, M J (1981), *Providence*, London, SCM.

Lucas, J R (1976), *Freedom and Grace*, London, SPCK, chapter 4.

Peacocke, A (1993), *Theology for a Scientific Age: being and becoming – natural, divine and human*, London, SCM, chapter 9.

Polkinghorne, J (1989), *Science and Providence*, London, SPCK.

Thomas, O C (ed.) (1983), *God's Activity in the World: the contemporary problem*, Chico, California, Scholars Press.

Ward, K (1990), *Divine Action*, London, Collins.

Ward, K (1996), *Religion and Creation*, Oxford, Oxford University Press, part III.

White, V (1985), *The Fall of a Sparrow: a concept of special divine action*, Exeter, Paternoster.

Wiles, M (1986), *God's Action in the World*, London, SCM.

Wiles, M (ed.) (1969), *Providence*, London, SPCK.

4. ACTS OF GOD: MIRACLES

Introduction

We turn now to the last of our six categories of God's activity.

Reflecting on experience
Try to repeat the reflection from the last chapter, but a notch higher up. Have there ever been any events in your own experience that you think of as *miraculous*? If so, what features marked them out for that label? If not, what sort of thing would have to happen for you to say, 'That was a miracle'?

Some people are more willing to use the language of miracle than others. Your response will partly depend on that fact. But it is also true that people live different lives and have different experiences, and that if miracles do happen they must in the nature of things be rare events.

Working on miracles

Miracles may be thought of as extreme examples of particular providence. The difference between the two concepts is that miracles are *usually* regarded as events that only happen when God overrides and overrules the natural order. Miracles are then defined as supernatural events that would not have happened if natural causes had simply run their course. Biblical examples of such divine 'interventions' include the parting of the Red Sea (Exodus 14:21–31) and Jesus' miracles of healing and his 'Nature miracles' (for example, Mark 4:35 to 5:43; John 4:46–54).

Remembering our analogy of the boat from Chapter 3, we may say that in the case of a miracle God 'the boatman' steers the boat out of the river altogether, transcending ('going beyond') the boundaries of the laws of Nature by 'pulling it across dry land'. Alternatively, on our other analogy, God 'the pianist' plays an anomalous ('irregular') note on the piano, one that is not part of a sequence or scale and seems unconnected with anything that went before; the note is therefore not just unexpected, but *unpredictable*.

Well, that is the usual view. But you may use the word 'miracle' differently.

EXERCISE

Here are some accounts of both unusual and everyday events. Which would *you* label as 'miraculous'? Consider:

1 the building in which you are sitting rises 20 metres above its foundations and then gently descends again;
2 the sun rises tomorrow morning;
3 it rains during your holiday;
4 the birth of a baby;
5 the birth of a deformed baby;
6 the conception of Jesus;
7 the birth of Jesus;
8 the Israelites cross the Red Sea dry-shod;
9 Jesus walks on the water;
10 the thirty ton jet flies across the Atlantic;
11 someone wins a lottery after they have prayed for money for themselves;
12 someone wins a lottery after they have prayed for money to give to charity;
13 someone is prevented by illness from going on a plane that later crashes;
14 a terrorist is killed in a freak car crash on his way to commit mass murder;
15 the resurrection of Jesus;
16 your survival or resurrection 'in heaven';
17 the patient with inoperable cancer recovers completely after his trip to Lourdes.

▶▶

Before reading further, try to make explicit the criteria you used in this exercise, by writing down your definition of a miracle. What do *you* mean when you call something a miracle?

Defining the miraculous

Most theologians argue that there are *two* aspects to the religious idea of a miracle. You may have noted them both in your own definition. A miracle is both *scientifically inexplicable* and *religiously significant*. Few of the examples in the exercise meet both these criteria.

If a miracle is an event for which no natural explanation can yet be offered, or for which any natural explanation would demand a drastic reconstruction of our present scientific knowledge, miracles are likely to be rare. How many of our examples fall into either of these categories? But to call something a miracle *also* implies that it gives rise to religious awe, wonder and gratitude. It is the absence of this second element that makes example 1 inappropriate as a candidate for the description 'miraculous'. If we were to add the qualification 'of moral worth' to the criterion 'religiously significant', we might have additional doubts about some of the other examples on the list, such as number 11. Miracles are now becoming even rarer!

But some religious thinkers emphasise the religious element *at the expense of* the element of scientific inexplicability. Thus for Paul Tillich a genuine miracle produces a numinous astonishment, points to the mystery of being and is received 'as a sign-event in an ecstatic experience', but all 'without contradicting the rational structure of reality' (Tillich, 1968, p. 130). More extremely, the great nineteenth-century theologian Friedrich Schleiermacher considered that *all events* were miracles because they could all evoke a sense of our dependence on God whether they could be scientifically explained or not. He wrote:

> Miracle is simply the religious name for event. Every event, even the most natural and usual, becomes a miracle, as soon as the religious view of it can be the dominant. To me all is miracle. In your sense the inexplicable and strange alone is miracle, in mine it is no miracle. The more religious you are, the more miracle would you see everywhere. (Schleiermacher, 1958, p. 88, cf. p. 114)

Others, however, insist on the element of surprise and 'wonderfulness' in the definition of miracle. For them, nothing counts as a miracle that is not a scientific oddity defying natural explanation.

EXERCISE

What are the strengths and weaknesses of these two approaches to defining the miraculous: the one that minimises and the other that insists on the scientific criterion? Which do you tend to side with, and why?

You might think that Schleiermacher's approach allows for a wide-ranging spirituality which finds God's hand everywhere. But has the word 'miracle' lost its point on this perspective? Those who consistently claim that everything is a miracle treat the word as a blanket term that has no determinate meaning, for there is nothing that we can then distinguish as not being a miracle.

The main problem with the other approach is that it may lead to our restricting our search for God to the inexplicable, ignoring the divine activity that is taking place all around us, in and through the laws of Nature. Ernst and Marie-Luise Keller have developed this critique:

> Christians who are always waiting for special revelations or dispensations or leadings from a heavenly world often prove to be blind towards the real world. The man whose gaze is directed towards a supernatural history and who looks for miracles and 'facts of salvation' is in constant danger of losing his eye for 'normal' history. (Keller and Keller, 1969, p. 245)

Further, this restricted spirituality has been denigrated as a 'God of the gaps' theology, vulnerable to the risk that God is 'driven progressively from the world' as science advances (Gunton, 1997, p. 152).

Other theological problems

Another criticism of a 'miraculous theology' is that (paradoxically) it calls into question God's power and skill. For why should an omnipotent, omniscient creator *need* to intervene in creation? Why has God not so ordered Nature that it does his will anyway? Are creation and providence not enough? One answer might be that God has to intervene when human beings thwart the divine plan with their own free, and therefore unpredictable, behaviour (see Chapters 3 and 7), or perhaps to exercise some control over the results of those indeterminate events within atoms.

What role can miracles play in Christian 'apologetics' (the branch of theology that argues the case for Christian belief)?

EXERCISE

Think about your unbelieving friends and ask yourself (or them!) whether they would be more likely to become Christians if you could first get them to acknowledge that miracles do happen.

Although miracles have been traditionally used as evidence for God's existence or activity, simply proving that certain unexplained events happened does not prove that *God* performed them. It may simply be that there are some inexplicable events in Nature that are not caused (or wholly determined) by other events. Such phenomena might evoke awe and wonder in us, but why propose a special sort of divine activity as the correct explanation for them?

Note also that if you try to defend the claim that miracles happen by saying that we do not yet know enough about the laws of Nature to be able to say categorically that these events 'break' such laws, you place yourself in a difficult position. For if the events do fall under some (presently unknown) natural explanation, then God's activity is not needed to account for them anyway.

The problem of evidence

David Hume argued that the evidence in favour of miracles must always be balanced against the evidence for the law of Nature to which the miracle is an exception. 'A miracle is a violation of the laws of nature; and as a firm and unalterable experience has established these laws, the proof against a miracle, from the very nature of the fact, is as entire as any argument from experience can possibly be imagined' (Hume, 1902, p. 114).

For Hume, the historical testimony in favour of the supposed miracle that Jesus 'walked on water' is always to be set in the scales against the evidence (in fact the human testimony) in favour of the law that heavy objects always sink in water. It is not surprising that on this test most accounts of miracles are rejected, especially those that would make a miracle 'a just foundation for any . . . system of religion', since (at least according to Hume) 'violations of truth are more common in the testimony concerning religious miracles' (pp. 127, 129). Like many

Enlightenment thinkers, Hume was very suspicious of the claims of religious people, and especially of religious authorities.

EXERCISE
What do you think of Hume's argument on miracles? Is this a reasonable position to take? Is it a *scientific* view?

Hume's criticisms are most clearly directed to the degree of credence we should give to the testimony of other people about miracles. But the situation is surely different if I witness a miracle myself, for it is much less plausible to say that I should then doubt the evidence of my own senses (and, perhaps, my memory). What Hume does show is that all *reports* of miracles begin at a profound disadvantage; for, judged by the rest of our experience of Nature and the human testimony that underlies its laws, the apparently miraculous event must be said to be improbable. This principle is used by historians whenever they attempt to reconstruct what happened in the past. Those reported miracles that imply fundamental disturbances of the expected order of Nature unquestionably 'require overwhelming evidence before we are disposed to accept them'. This explains the proper 'scientific prejudice against the conception of miracle' (Hesse, 1965, p. 41).

Science, by virtue of its method, is incapable of recognising miracles. The scientist must always look for a scientific (natural) explanation. If he fails to find one he will report that failure, but that is as far as he can go. The inhabitants of a two-dimensional universe would experience a three-dimensional missile passing through their world as a series of events apparently uncaused by anything else in their field of view. They would not be able to say where it comes from or whither it goes. Science, similarly, cannot comment on any supernatural dimension which may underlie, or interact with, the causal web of the world. It can know nothing of it, and must remain puzzled by its effects. But Hume's argument, as he himself acknowledged (despite occasional lapses of consistency), does not rule out the possibility of a miracle ever taking place.

Interpreting intervention

The Christian's belief in general and particular providence does not conflict with scientific claims, but it does deny their ultimacy as a description of everything that happens. Science can only describe and predict events in the world; the theological doctrine of providence adds a theological 'third dimension' to these scientific claims. Belief in miracles, however, seems to be in conflict with any notion of 'inviolable' laws of Nature.

If scientific laws can be formulated without exceptions, then the scientist must regard a miracle as a 'violation' of such laws. However, because of the 'quantum indeterminacy' within the atom, the laws of science are now generally regarded as statistical generalisations concerning what happens in the world, rather than rigid universal laws. So miracles, as non-repeatable exceptions to these laws, cannot be ruled out from the outset, although they must still be regarded as highly improbable. Yet it is logically possible (that is, it makes sense to say) that such 'physically impossible' events *might* happen.

The laws of Nature are the best accounts we can have of the way Nature behaves, and they therefore serve as rules for predicting what will most probably happen in the future. We must accept them and rely on them; but we can at the same time allow that occasional and unpredictable interventions could happen that 'break' these laws. There is a better way of putting this. It has been said that a miracle does not violate but is 'outside' the laws of Nature, in the way that a royal or presidential pardon is outside the laws of a state. A pardon is not 'illegal' and forms no part of the system of law, yet it has legal consequences (Purtill, 1978, pp. 69–71). Miracles have a similar status.

So far I have been using the word 'intervention' quite recklessly to label God's miraculous activity. It is a term that is also open to criticism, however, both for suggesting that God is not involved with the world unless and until he 'intervenes', and for implying that this intervention is some sort of intrusion, interference or manipulation from outside. Most believers do not picture God as an external, interfering agent correcting the unfortunate consequences of Nature's causal pathways. And most scientists now consider Nature to be an open, flexible, emergent system (particularly at the subatomic level), not a closed deterministic machine. Many theologians would therefore argue that it is neither an intervention nor a violation if God determines particular events within the limits allowed by the structure of scientific laws *that have openness built in to them already*, by guiding the universe 'by purposive choices among its alternative pathways' (Ward, 1990, pp. 79, 69; cf. Pollard, 1958, but contrast Peacocke, 1993, pp. 152–157). As the Church of England's Doctrine Commission once put it: 'Necessarily the Spirit's action is hidden within the cloudiness of the intrinsically unpredictable' (1991, p. 142).

The difference between providence and miracles, then, is perhaps only one of the *degree* of God's activity, with the resulting effects being more spectacular in the case of a miracle, as they are (apparently) 'beyond Nature'. Even in the case of these more overt influences, however, many are reluctant to speak of a transgression of Nature or a violation of the true character of things, but rather of 'the raising of an object beyond its natural powers of operation, so as to show its supernatural origin' (Ward, 1990, p. 181).

Answers to prayer

A number of theological problems concerning providence and miracle come into clear focus in discussion about 'answers to prayer'. Christians often speak of God answering 'petitionary' prayers (those in which we ask God for things) in one of two ways:

• by strengthening the concern of the person who prays and her determination to act on the basis of that concern;
• by helping the person who prays to accept whatever happens as God's will.

We may think of these as spiritual or psychological 'answers' and wonder whether God is needed to effect them. The belief that this is all there is to prayer is well-captured in Dewi Phillips' book *The Concept of Prayer*:

> Medical treatment has failed, and a child is dying. Religious parents pray, 'O God, let her live'. What does this amount to? The parents recognise that things can go either way; the child may live or it may die ... But they meet the possibility of things going either way in God. They recognise their own helplessness, that the way things go is beyond their control, and seek something to sustain them which does not depend on the way things go, namely, the love of God. (Phillips, 1965, p. 120)

All true petitionary prayer here reduces to the petition, 'Thy will be done.'

But others might make an additional appeal: to God's providential activity or miraculous intervention to answer the prayer. Peter Baelz writes: 'our asking in faith may make it possible for God to do something which he could not have done without our asking' (Baelz,

1968, p. 118). This additional effect of prayer may be thought of in various ways:

- our prayer may change God's intentions;
- our prayer may give God a sufficient reason for acting that he did not have before;
- our prayer '"releases" paranormal forces of some kind' (Price, 1972, p. 55).

We may still wonder why God's activity should depend on our prayers. Eleanore Stump argues that the great value of making prayerful requests is that they allow us to have a relationship with God that neither spoils nor dominates us (Stump, 1979).

Yet the traditional interpretation of 'physical' answers to prayer is rejected by many contemporary believers, who prefer to pray for 'mental and spiritual' effects in themselves and others. Some will reason that it implies 'less of an intervention' for God to influence human minds and hearts, by strengthening our wills or giving wisdom to our doctors, than it would for God to interrupt the causal laws of the physical world. But we have seen that the concept of an omnipotent creator implies that God *could* perform miracles and answer prayer miraculously if God wishes so to do.

However, the believer must then face the question, 'Why does God not do so more often, and to better effect?'

EXERCISE

Imagine yourself questioned in this way by an agnostic. What answer could you offer to the question: 'Why does God not more often perform miracles and intervene in the world in answer to prayer?'

One response might be that if God performed *too many* miracles or interventions our confidence in the whole order of Nature (an order that we rely on to survive) would soon disappear. But John Habgood points out the moral problem of the selective nature of miracles: 'No doubt ... it is not for us to judge what is morally appropriate and what is not. But an unbeliever cannot be blamed for wondering why a God who can reserve parking spaces for his chosen ones could not divert a few Nazi death trains' (Habgood, 1986, p. 111). David Jenkins, Habgood's successor as Bishop of Durham, notoriously declared that a

God who engaged in selective miracle-working was a 'cultic idol . . . a false and misdeveloped picture of the true and gracious God' (Jenkins, 1987, p. 5).

This debate is part of the problem of evil, which we shall explore in the next two chapters.

An expectant spirit?

In the end, our understanding of prayer must connect with our understanding of Christian *spirituality* and this brings us back to the doctrine of providence. An emphasis on miracle and particular providence may lead us to embrace a spirituality that expects God to act and even to intervene to help us. A focus on general providence, however, encourages our 'self-abandonment' and spiritual patience. At its best this second perspective reminds us that 'the LORD gave, and the LORD has taken away; blessed be the name of the LORD' (Job 1:21 NRSV), but at its worst it fosters 'mere resignation' and even fatalism (Migliore, 1991, pp. 116–117).

Different traditions of Christian spirituality may agree that God is in control, but expect different expressions of that control and different things to happen in God's world. Different people are attracted by these different styles of spirituality. What about you?

Further reading

Introductory

Baelz, P (1982), *Does God Answer Prayer?*, London, Darton, Longman and Todd.

Habgood, J (1986), Discovering God in action, in T Moss (ed.), *In Search of Christianity*, pp. 108–120, London, Waterstone.

Jenkins, D (1987), *God, Miracle and the Church of England*, London, SCM.

Moule, C F D (ed.) (1965), *Miracles: Cambridge studies in their philosophy and history*, London, Mowbray.

Peterson, M, Hasker, W, Reichenbach, B and Basinger, D (1991), *Reason and Religious Belief*, New York, Oxford University Press, chapter 9.

Ramsey, I T (1971), *Our Understanding of Prayer*, London, SPCK.

Vardy, P (1990), *The Puzzle of God*, London, Collins, chapters 15 to 17.

Advanced

Baelz, P (1968), *Prayer and Providence*, London, SCM.

Brümmer, V (1984), *What Are We Doing When We Pray?* London, SCM.

Davies, B (1985), *Thinking about God*, London, Chapman, chapters 2 and 11.

Davies, B (1993), *An Introduction to the Philosophy of Religion*, Oxford, Oxford University Press, chapter 10.

Geivett, R D and Habermas, G R (eds) (1997), *In Defence of Miracles: a comprehensive case for God's action in history*, Leicester, Apollos.

Keller, E and Keller, M-L (1969), *Miracles in Dispute*, ET London, SCM.

Lewis, C S (1960), *Miracles*, London, Collins.

Moore, G (1988), *Believing in God*, Edinburgh, T and T Clark, chapters 6 and 7.

Phillips, D Z (1965), *The Concept of Prayer*, London, Routledge and Kegan Paul.

(See also the further reading for Chapter 3.)

5. THE CHALLENGES OF SCIENCE

Introduction

We are often told that we live in a scientific and technological age. The technology is not in doubt; it is an increasingly pervasive influence in all of our lives. But just how 'scientific' are we?

The level of understanding of science varies greatly in the adult population and people adopt different attitudes to the methods and discoveries of science. The extent to which you think that science is in conflict with religious belief may well influence how you think both of science and of religion.

Reflecting on experience
How do you view the relationship between science and religion? Which areas of your own religious belief have been challenged by the work of scientists? How have you tried to resolve these challenges in your own mind?

Science and religion: conflict or complement?

Most probably you included in your list of challenges the conflict between biblical and evolutionary accounts of the origins of living things, especially human beings. Remembering the theme of the last chapter, the problem of miracles probably also came to mind. The accounts of contemporary physicists about the origins of the universe could also pose difficulties for your theology.

We shall look at some of these challenges and how they might be answered in this chapter. But it is useful at this point to say a word about the science/religion debate in general.

The conventional account of the fundamental relationship between science and religion is of a state of warfare. But this is now challenged by many historians of science and writers on science and religion. Although Greek philosophers, through their search for a wisdom of explanation, may be said to have initiated the reflection on Nature that developed into science, it was *theological* considerations that allowed the rise of an empirical science based on observing Nature and manipulating it through experiments. These factors included the recognition of the relative independence and 'contingency' (non-necessity) of the universe and the conviction that it was designed by a divine mind – and was therefore orderly – but was not itself divine.

EXERCISE

Traditionally, Christians have treated Nature as a sort of *book*. It has been said that there are two books that can tell you about God: the Bible, the book of God's words, and Nature, the book of God's works. Both have the same author and we need diligently and intelligently to search out God's mind in both (cf. Peacocke, 1979, chapter I).

Try to develop this image of the two books and unpack its implications for the science/religion debate. How useful do you find it?

The analogy is not perfect (analogies never are). The book of Nature tells us a lot about Nature but it does not say who wrote it. Another book is needed for that – a book that contains some sort of revelation. With *its* help Nature looks very different.

Nothing in Nature is really 'explained' by this second book but it might help by promoting the intellectual contentment that comes from adopting a different perspective on Nature. Revelation helps us to set Nature in context – a context that includes us (Polkinghorne, 1994, pp. 36–37). Our *attitude* to Nature may then be changed and that makes it more likely that our *behaviour* towards Nature will be changed.

Creation with attitude

We might try our hand here at developing a 'spirituality of creation'. If Nature is evaluated as 'very good' (Genesis 1:31), and treated as a gift from God, then attitudes of gratitude, esteem and respect may be evoked as an appropriate response. As we saw in Chapter 2, the doctrine of creation has usually been taken as denying that matter is evil. Indeed it encourages a *celebration* of the body and the world, of 'muck and matter'.

Some people despise science for the way it concentrates on the 'things of the earth' rather than the 'life of the mind'. But true religion is like true science (and true life) in that it gets its hands dirty. Both science and religion consider the lilies of the field and the fowls of the air; they rejoice in them and learn from them. Both of them recognise that all human existence is an in-the-world existence and that we are ourselves a part of Nature. We are embodied selves, and the best theology acknowledges that we were created and intended as such; we are not angels who have got stuck in the mud by accident.

EXERCISE

One of the saddest aspects of the rejection of evolution that is encouraged by 'creationists' is their attempt to reintroduce a radical distinction between *homo sapiens* and other animals (see Kitcher, 1983). In the nineteenth century, Darwin's theory was treated with most abhorrence over this issue, for the doctrine of special creation had given human beings a dignity that the theory of evolution threatened to take away.

📖 **Read Genesis 1:26–27 and 2:4–7, 18–24; Psalm 8; Isaiah 2:5–22.**

What status does the Bible give to human beings?

The biblical view of the dignity of human beings is deeply paradoxical. In Genesis *Adam* (Hebrew for 'the man') is a pun on the Hebrew for 'earth' or 'ground', *adhamah*. Humankind is made from the dust of the earth. We are created out of flesh and bone, DNA and protein, sugars and amino acids, molecules and atoms, and – deeper down among the elementary particles – quarks and leptons. Yet humankind is also made but a 'little less than God', as Psalm 8:5 puts it. The dignity of being called to be co-workers with God, God's trustees, the recipients of God's revelation and the bearers of God's image, is therefore not incompatible with our more earthy origins. Since we share a common origin with the beasts, we need not feel ashamed to be animals or to feel close to animals. As we study them through the sciences we should expect to learn more about ourselves.

And *religion* can help us to develop appropriate attitudes towards this world that science explores.

> Perhaps the sciences adopt an objective set of attitudes to the world, seeking to describe its observable features dispassionately and neutrally. Religious discourse may express a reactive response to the world, as emotionally responded to and affectively engaged with. But it is the same world to which these attitudes are being directed. (Ward, 1996b, p. 120)

Despite frequent criticisms to the contrary, scientists on the whole treat Nature with a sort of secular awe and reverence. Richard Dawkins has made a plea for 'good poetic science', 'science inspired by a poetic sense of wonder', arguing that the spirit of wonder that inspired the poets 'is the very same spirit that moves great scientists' (Dawkins, 1998, pp. xii, 27). Einstein implied much more than this, in characterising every 'true searcher' of Nature as having 'a kind of religious reverence' for its masterly order and harmony (Polkinghorne, 1986, p. 63). Wonder and reverence have an ethical dimension, and the majority of scientists appreciate their responsibility towards Nature and their participation within it. These attitudes mirror the believers' awe at God's handiwork and their sense of being guardians and trustees of a gift that is beyond their deserving.

Getting the level right

EXERCISE

Consider these two quotations:

Children should be informed that there are *two conflicting views on origins: some* scientists believe in evolution, others in special creation. The arguments on *both* sides should be presented, and children should be *free to choose* between them. (The creationist D C C Watson, quoted in Kitcher, 1983, pp. 174–175)

Strictly speaking, evolution has nothing to do with 'creation' itself . . . Creation is the term that describes the miracle of ▶▶

---

existence itself . . . there is in principle no contradiction between creation and evolution. The concepts belong on different levels. They are talking about different sides of the same reality. (Moltmann, 1985, p. 196)

What do you make of these claims?

The 'conflict between science and religion' is in the main a debate between the explanations (findings, theories) offered by science and those offered by the doctrines (beliefs, revelations) of religion. These conflicts usually arise when the explanations are taken to be at the same level.

Explanation in science is largely about success in making predictions, which is the result of bringing the events of Nature under some sort of law that we can use to answer the question, 'What would happen if . . . ?' But religious belief does not work at that level. If it is properly interpreted, the doctrine of creation can accommodate almost any science. Practically any account of the origin of the universe and the origin of species will do, for theology is about that which lies below and beyond the physics and the biology and is appropriately termed the '*meta*physical' (*meta* is Greek for 'after'). It is not another, competing scientific explanation of the origins of things. Armed with the doctrine of continuous creation, then, the theist need not be fazed by any scientific explanation. Whenever science proposes an account of the development of the physical universe or of biological life, the believer can always add 'and God sustains all this'.

Therefore at the level of ultimate explanation there is no conflict – or at least no straightforward contradiction – between science and religion. It is only when we insist on coming down to a more specific (or more 'superficial') level of theological explanation that the sciences become a problem. Thus a belief in the evolution of species over billions of years, and a belief in the special separate creation of every species over several days, are two particular explanations that conflict because they operate at the same level. We can usually solve such problems only by shifting the level at which we do theology – taking it back to its rightful place.

As we saw in Chapter 1, the disciplines of science and theology answer different questions about the origin of things and the diversity of life. Science reveals what the world is like; theology asks 'meta questions' about its purpose. If Genesis does not offer us an alternative *scientific* account (and how could it, if it was written well before the development of scientific thinking?), then there is no conflict between the biblical and the scientific stories of creation.

We turn now to look at the theological relevance of some particular scientific claims in physics and biology concerning phenomena both great and small.

Cosmology and relativity

According to many modern physicists, the universe probably originated in a 'singularity', a point in space-time at which its curvature was infinite. Energy and matter arose from this, exploding in the gigantic thermo-nuclear 'Big Bang'. For theists, God is responsible for that origin, as well as for sustaining in existence all that flows from it. The only theological issues raised here are the well-worn questions as to how God can be a *cause* 'before' there was any time and how a timeless God can *act* at all. If God is 'in time', even though not in our time, these questions are more easily answered.

Einstein's special and general theories of relativity destroy the view that time is a universal absolute, for it goes more slowly at higher speeds and in strong gravitational fields. There is no universal 'now'. This can lead to a sort of relativ*ism*, in which our accounts of reality are recognised as being from a particular perspective, framework and standpoint. Theology needs to come to terms with this emphasis on the importance of the human perspective in our knowledge.

Some physicists have developed a sort of secular version of the 'Argument to Design' (the claim that the adaptation we find in the world points to a designer God) in the so-called 'Anthropic Principle'. In its weak form, this holds that we can only observe a universe whose existence is consistent with our presence as observers. This is a trivial, self-evident truth. In its strong form, however, as adopted by Brandon Carter and others, the principle claims that the universe must be such as to admit conscious beings in at some stage: that the universe possesses many of its properties *because* they are necessary for the existence of our life and of observers.

Underlying such assertions is the recognition that the basic physical constants in Nature (the expansion rate of the universe, the relative strength of the nuclear forces, the particle/anti-particle ratio, etc.) are 'just right' to allow for the possibility of the formation of planets and of life. This evidence is so abundant that 'it is hard to resist the impression that the present structure of the universe . . . has been rather carefully thought out' (Davies, 1984, p. 189).

But isn't this just a lucky chance? After all, if Nature were *not* like this we would not be here to be so impressed! Is this universe so unlikely that it *must* have been designed?

The ten card trick

EXERCISE

Richard Swinburne offers an intriguing parable (Swinburne, 1979, p. 138). Imagine that someone imprisons you in a room with a machine that randomly shuffles ten packs of playing cards simultaneously. 'You will be safe if the first draw consists of an ace of hearts from every pack,' he informs you. 'Otherwise a bomb will be detonated.' He sets the machine running and leaves. And lo! It deals an ace of hearts from each pack.

Does this mean that the machine must have been rigged? (The chance of this deal happening *accidentally* is one in 144,555,105,949,000,000.) But is the result so fishy? After all, if any other combination had been dealt you would not be there to wonder at it.

What do you think?

We shall explore some of these issues later. But we should note here that a number of physicists maintain that there may be a sort of logical necessity about the way the world is, or that the complex cosmic order and 'fine-tuned' physical constants can be explained as arising from an initial state that is not particularly special. On other – admittedly very bizarre – accounts, *many* universes exist: perhaps many quantum worlds in parallel forever coming into existence, or multiple disconnected domains of space-time. It is then more plausible to argue that the existence of a universe that can sustain life might be a matter of chance alone.

Indeterminacy in Nature

Quantum mechanics is the branch of physics that explores the nature of reality at its smallest and most basic level. It leads to some weird conclusions. (The physicist Neils Bohr is reported as saying that anyone who is not shocked by quantum theory has not understood it.) The world at the subatomic level runs counter to common sense. Electrons, for example, behave sometimes like waves and sometimes like particles.

There also appears to be an intrinsic unpredictability within Nature. Certainly, we cannot *know* both the position and the momentum of subatomic particles. As a result, science's earlier picture of a completely deterministic universe has been replaced by an account of statistical approximations at the macro-level which hide an intrinsically surprising world within the atom. Despite Einstein's resistance to the claim, God *does* appear to 'play dice'.

It is this indeterminacy that some interpret as allowing God the freedom to steer Nature providentially at the quantum micro-level, without affecting the grosser macro-laws of causation. Perhaps indeterminacy also leaves room for human freedom (see Chapter 7), but let us note that 'a breech of causality does not in itself yield a significant concept of freedom; uncaused action would be chaotic and random, not at all what we mean by responsible choice' (Barbour, 1966, p. 309).

At a different physical level altogether, chaos theory recognises that the behaviour even of many large scale ('Newtonian') systems, such as the weather or evolutionary change, may be impossible to predict over any length of time. This is the famous 'butterfly effect'. An insect's tiny wing movements *could* eventually give rise to a hurricane thousands of miles away. We may need to think again even about God's ability to predict the future (see Chapter 3). But we can also claim that 'as far as physics is concerned, it is quite possible for God to influence the outcome of physical events, within certain limits, in ways undetectable by us', whether or not quantum uncertainty is fundamental to Nature (Ward, 1996a, p. 81).

Evolution

Many Christians are content to read the Genesis narratives as story-theology or 'myth'. A myth is like a parable; it is not literally true, scientifically or historically (there never was a Good Samaritan), but it contains a deep truth about the relationship between God and the world. (See another book in this series, Evans, 1999, pp. 78–80.)

Langdon Gilkey writes that most contemporary theologians would say that plants, animals and human beings have been created by God 'through evolution', but they also maintain that this biological truth about human beings 'does not produce a total understanding'. 'Evolution is accepted as a scientific concept, but like all such it is regarded as neither in conflict with nor determinative of theological concepts' (Gilkey, 1968, p. 170).

EXERCISE

Darwin's theory of evolution through 'the natural selection of chance variations', supplemented by the science of genetics, has provided a powerful framework for understanding life. But it also gives rise to a number of serious *theological problems* about God and the world.

What problems does the theory of evolution pose for your religious belief?

You might have come up with some of the following issues, in addition to questions about the nature of the biblical narratives (on this topic see another book in this series: Strange, 2000, chapter 4).

• The Argument to Design is now more difficult to mount. Evolution explains the adaptation of living things by reference to a combination of *chance* (genetic mutation, the 'chance recombination' of genes in sexual reproduction, and unpredictable changes in the environment) *plus necessity* ('the struggle for life' inevitably favouring some variations rather than others). The origin of variation within a species is unrelated to the survival needs of that species: in that sense such variations arise 'by chance'. Further, natural selection is a 'blind, unconscious, automatic process': no more than a 'blind watchmaker' in the production of the complex mechanisms of life (Dawkins, 1988, p. 5). But theologians are sometimes willing to speak of chance as 'the search radar of God, sweeping through all possible targets available to its probing', and to see it as an expression of 'the overflow of the divine generosity' (Peacocke, 1979, pp. 95, 111) on which God's laws of natural selection act. Others add that God does not leave the outcome entirely to chance and necessity (see below).

- The problem of natural evil is surely made worse by a process that caused Darwin himself to describe Nature as 'clumsy, wasteful, blundering, low, and horribly cruel' (Darwin, 1856). 'If God watches the sparrow fall, God must do so from a great distance', writes Holmes Rolston, adding that Nature itself is 'cruciform' (1987, p. 140; cf. Chapter 6 below).
- As we have seen, the blurring of the human/animal distinction in evolution challenges our human dignity. 'Sociobiology' or 'evolutionary psychology' seeks to explain human behaviour and our moral sense in terms of the forces of evolution. Should theology accept these explanations or resist them?
- Where does the evolutionary account of the 'Origin of Man' leave the doctrine of 'the Fall of Adam' (see Chapter 7)?

Evolution and providence

Many theologians argue that God has designed the laws and operations of Nature, including those of evolution, so that conscious beings would evolve. On this account, God is not thought of as further influencing or interfering with Nature, which develops autonomously. Others, however, regard the evolution of consciousness and rationality as too unlikely an outcome under these circumstances. They therefore argue that God exercises active causality in this area, rather than just passively allowing natural laws to run their course. This is not regarded as 'interference', but rather as a continuing causal influence of God on the appropriate events of Nature – particularly on events such as the mutation of genes that may not be *wholly* determined by other causes. As the ultimate spiritual environment for Nature, God can provide 'influencing constraints on the way it unfolds its inherent potentialities' (Ward, 1996a, p. 80, cf. chapter 7), perhaps by a type of 'top-down' causation in which the system-as-a-whole influences its parts more broadly, through a flow of information rather than energy (Peacocke, 1993, pp. 157–165).

Biochemistry

'Vitalists', who postulated a mysterious life force over and above the physics and chemistry of organisms, have been the losers in the history of biology. Yet many scientists now reject a reductionist account of life, arguing that life (and possibly mind) should be viewed as 'emergent qualities' of organised matter, dependent on a certain level of organisation of simpler parts. If there is a hierarchy of levels of organisation, there may also be distinctive laws and phenomena at the higher levels. This more 'holistic' view is opposed to the 'atomistic view' of the prejudice of materialism (the assertion that only matter exists). (On this topic, see Peacocke, 1979; O'Hear, 1989, chapter 8; Ward, 1990, chapter 4 and 1996a.)

Further reading

Introductory

Farrer, A (1966), *A Science of God?* London, Bles.

McGrath, A E (1999), *Science and Religion: an introduction*, Oxford, Blackwell.

Montenat, C, Plateaux, L and Roux, P (1985), *How to Read the World: creation in evolution*, ET London, SCM.

Poole, M (1995), *Beliefs and Values in Science Education*, Buckingham, Open University Press.

Tilby, A (1992), *Science and the Soul: new cosmology, the self and God*, London, SPCK.

Wilkinson, D (1996), *God, The Big Bang and Stephen Hawking*, Crowborough, Monarch.

Advanced

Barbour, I G (1966), *Issues in Science and Religion*, London, SCM.

Barbour, I G (1990), *Religion in an Age of Science*, London, SCM.

Davies, P (1984), *God and the New Physics*, Harmondsworth, Penguin.

Jaki, S (1986), *Science and Creation*, Edinburgh, Scottish Academic Press.

McGrath, A E (1998), *The Foundations of Dialogue in Science and Religion*, Oxford, Blackwell.

Peacocke, A R (1979), *Creation and the World of Science*, Oxford, Oxford University Press.

Peacocke, A (1993), *Theology for a Scientific Age: being and becoming – natural, divine and human*, London, SCM.

Polkinghorne, J (1996), *Serious Talk: science and religion in dialogue*, London, SCM.

Polkinghorne, J (1998), *Science and Theology: an introduction*, London, SPCK.

Richardson, W M and Wildman, W J (eds) (1996), *Religion and Science: history, method, dialogue*, London, Routledge.

Rolston, H (1987), *Science and Religion: a critical survey*, New York, Random House.

Southgate, C (ed.) (1999), *God, Humanity and the Cosmos: a textbook in science and religion*, Edinburgh, T and T Clark.

Ward, K (1996), *God, Chance and Necessity*, Oxford, Oneworld.

Ward, K (1996), *Religion and Creation*, Oxford, Clarendon, chapter 12.

6. THE PROBLEMS OF SUFFERING

Introduction

In this chapter and the next we tackle the area of greatest difficulty for Christian belief, the problem of evil. We begin, as usual, with your reflections.

Reflecting on experience

Think of a concrete example from a current news story of a situation in which people have suffered. Reflect on:
- the nature of that suffering (physical pain, mental anguish);
- its cause and status (caused by Nature, by human intention or by accident; 'deserved' or not, 'avoidable' or not); and
- its consequences for the sufferers and others (all the consequences being bad or the suffering leading to a good 'end' that would justify the situation as a 'means' towards it).

What would you say to the people involved in this situation if they asked, 'Why does God allow this?'

How do you understand God's relationship to *your own* suffering? Think about a recent situation of physical pain or mental suffering that has afflicted you directly. In particular, reflect on:
- the extent you think God was responsible; and
- the human and Christian resources, thoughts and actions that might (or did) help you through it.

Christian education and theological thinking result from a conversation between our reflection on our own experience and our reflection on the

Christian tradition. At this point you might find it illuminating to listen to part of that tradition in the light of your own experience.

EXERCISE

📖 **Read Job chapters 1 to 3, then 4:7– 11 and 5:17–27** (Eliphaz's speech), **chapters 6 and 21** (Job's response), **and chapters 9 to 10** (Job's dispute against God).

How would you characterise Job's reaction (or reactions) to his suffering? What do you think of Eliphaz's comments?

In fact, the Book of Job really comprises two books: an early prose story of the 'patient Job' who is rewarded for his patience (chapters 1, 2 and 42:7–17), and a later poem (3:1 to 42:6) in which Job challenges God with the injustice of his situation, criticises the explanations of his friends, and finally hears God's rebuke from the whirlwind (38:1 to 42:6). The whole text is essential reading for anyone seeking a biblical perspective on suffering. We shall refer to it again later.

The problems of evil

There are two rather different senses in which evil is a 'problem' for the religious believer.

First, there is the 'practical' or 'existential' problem of what we can do – and what God does – to overcome evil. In part this is the spiritual and religious, or psychological and pastoral, problem of *coping with evil* in our own lives, perhaps with the help of meditation, prayer, worship, friendships and fellowship, and so on. The question about God that is posed here is, 'Is this a God who can help?'

Second, there is also a 'theoretical' or 'intellectual' (sometimes called 'the theological') problem of evil, which is the problem of *explaining evil* in God's creation. The question here is, 'Is belief in God intelligible in a world that contains evil?'

Much theological writing on this subject is concerned with the second problem rather than the first. 'Theodicy' is the name for that part of theology that deals with the intellectual problem of evil and attempts to show that God is just despite the evil of the world.

Can we separate the theoretical from the spiritual problems of evil so clearly? And how can we be sure that we are developing a *Christian* theodicy, rather than just a general defence of belief in God? Diogenes Allen writes that in considering the problem of evil we should begin with Christ's affliction, the most severe and greatest evil, and relate this to the love of God. 'It is what is unique and central to Christianity which allows us to conceive of all suffering as the presence of God to us through the world (both natural and social), and enables us to find God's love in and through the events of this life' (Allen, 1990, p. 207).

Other Christians are unhappy with the abstract philosophical tone of arguments that seek to justify suffering or defend God, in the context of 'solutions' to an intellectual problem. Donald MacKinnon writes:

> It is sheer nonsense to speak of the Christian religion as offering a solution of the problem of evil. . . . To suggest that Christianity deals with the problem of evil by encouraging the believer to view it from a cosmic perspective is totally to misunderstand both the difficulty and the consolation of its treatment. Rather Christianity takes the history of Jesus and urges the believer to find, in the endurance of the ultimate contradictions of human existence that belongs to its very substance, the assurance that in the worst that can befall his creatures, the creative Word keeps company with those whom he has called his own. 'Is it nothing unto you all ye that pass by? Behold and consider whether there be any sorrow like unto my sorrow.' (MacKinnon, 1968, pp. 92–93)

EXERCISE
What would *you* mean by a Christian 'solution' to the problem of suffering? Does an *explanation* of evil (explaining its cause and justifying its existence) help people to *cope* with it? And if this is so, should such explanations be offered at the time, as part of our ministry of pastoral care?

When Job's friends arrived to comfort him, they first simply wept with him. They sat with him on the ground seven days and nights 'and no one spoke to him, for they saw that his suffering was very great' (Job 2:13 NRSV). In the text as we now have it, they *later* begin to offer their own explanations of his suffering – explanations which do not satisfy or 'comfort' Job, and which even seem to be rejected by God (42:7). Perhaps explanations are out of place in pastoral contexts like this?

There must surely be some role, however, for the more 'theoretical' or 'intellectual' type of theodicy in Christian life and thought. The rest of this chapter will attempt to review a number of these explanatory theodicies.

Biblical theodicy

There are many references in Scripture to the origin and explanation of evil, in addition to those in the Book of Job.

EXERCISE
📖 **Read Genesis 3; Psalm 37; Ezekiel 18; John 9:1–5; Luke 13: 1–5; Romans 8:18–30; Hebrews 4:14–16.**

Make notes summarising the range of attempts in the Old Testament to explain human suffering, and the New Testament's development of some of these explanations and its challenge to others.

You may care to have these notes to hand when reading the rest of this chapter. I only comment here that the New Testament, and Christian tradition generally, mostly seeks to understand evil in the light of Jesus' life and death ('the theology of the cross'), seen in some sense as a victory over evil and a reversal of the rebellion of Adam. In Christ, God somehow enters his creation and is able there both to experience the force of evil and to overcome it (see Moltmann, 1974, chapter 6). These insights must form the backdrop to any attempt at a Christian theodicy.

Defining evil

'Evil' is 'that which ought not to be' (Hick, 1983b, p. 93). It is the term we adopt for what human beings avoid and disapprove of, and what we think they ought to avoid and disapprove of.

But what sort of things are evil? And is the answer to that question just a matter of opinion? If it is, we will not need a theodicy at all. Despite many areas of disagreement, however, people on the whole do agree in denouncing at least some examples of pain, suffering or cruelty.

To call a situation or act evil is to say that in and of itself it is a bad thing (it is 'intrinsically' evil). This is true even if it leads to other good things (when we may say that it is also 'instrumentally' good), or if it is part of a larger good situation. Theological discussion of the problem of evil frequently distinguishes two principal types of evil:

- *Natural evil* or *physical evil* covers events of Nature (disease, famine, floods, etc.) that cause (physical) pain and (mental) suffering.
- *Moral evil* labels human wrongdoing and the pain and suffering that it causes.

In these discussions, calling a situation evil does not imply that any *agent* is responsible for it or intended it (or intended it to be evil). Earthquakes may be described as evil even though no one – not even God, perhaps – causes them. Nevertheless, some writers *do* distinguish between 'the problem of evil' (meaning the problem of moral evil) and 'the problem of suffering' (natural evil).

This chapter is mainly devoted to a consideration of the suffering caused by Nature; the next chapter concerns human sin.

Defining the intellectual problem of evil

The difficulty faced by the Christian in explaining evil may be presented quite bluntly. Either God cannot abolish evil or he will not. If God cannot, then he is not all powerful; if God will not, then he is not all good.

What problem?

All problems of explanation are only problems in a given context. If a friend arrives at your front door dressed as an armadillo that will constitute a 'problem', unless you are going with her to a fancy dress party. The existence of evil only constitutes a problem that demands some explanation in the context of certain *beliefs* about God and the world.

We may explore that belief-context further by breaking down the challenge of evil to theological thinking into six statements, as follows:

- Evil exists.
- There is only God, who is the supreme creator of everything out of nothing (see Chapter 2).
- God is all knowing ('omniscient' – God can know everything that can be known) and all powerful ('omnipotent' – God can do anything that can be done).
- God is all loving ('infinitely, perfectly good').

- An omniscient and omnipotent God must
  (a) *know* about all evil and know how to prevent all evil, and
  (b) *be able* to prevent all evil.
- An all loving God must *wish* to prevent all evil.

  In order to solve the theological problem of evil at least one of these propositions must be rejected. But which of them can the Christian believer actually deny?

EXERCISE
Taking each of the six statements in turn, try to think of an account of God's relationship to humans that might allow us to deny that statement, and yet still call ourselves Christian.

Some 'easy answers'

We could quickly solve the problem of evil by accepting one of the following claims. Unfortunately, most Christian believers would disown all of them. You might reflect on why that is and whether you agree that none of them is acceptable.

'There is no God'

If God does not exist, there is no need to find an explanation for evil. Atheists do not have an *intellectual* problem of evil, although they too must cope with it.

'Evil is not real'

In some Eastern religions evil is treated as illusion *(maya)*, along with the whole world of sense experience. It is not 'really' there at all, and we must achieve this insight if we are ever to escape the power of the illusion. Christian Scientists also hold that pain is an illusion. But the Bible always treats both evil and the world as fully real. In any case, we might say that 'to suffer from an illusion' of this kind is itself a type of suffering.

'God is not completely good'

Some religions believe that God is a mixture of good and evil. Thus in the Hindu Shaivite tradition, principles of both good and evil exist together in one divine source. Christians, however, claim that God is perfect.

'There is an evil god'

This solution is proposed by those dualistic religions in which good is the creation of a good god but evil derives from an evil god; both gods have a similar status and neither is responsible for the other's existence. This conviction is to be found, at least on some interpretations, in the Zoroastrian 'ultimate dualism' between Ahura Mazda (the Wise Lord) and the Hostile Spirit. The same answer to the problem is found in those faiths that believe in many gods (polytheism), as well as in those that believe in a 'creator' who works on pre-existing evil matter that he did not create to form the world. (Note that belief in the Devil, in Christianity and some other faiths, does not represent such an ultimate dualism – see Chapter 7.)

'God is limited'

A 'finite God' would not be able to prevent evil because he could never be in absolute control, by contrast with the unlimited ('infinite') God of traditional Christian theology. In addition to the examples already offered, this view is held by most 'process theologians', who think of God as 'persuading' rather than 'controlling' the events of the world (see Chapter 8). There is continuing controversy whether the denial of omnipotence can be regarded as orthodox. Many more religious thinkers are willing to deny God's omniscience (see Chapter 3).

More complex views

There is no single explanation of evil within the Christian tradition. The following attempts have achieved wide circulation, while remaining contentious.

'Some pain is inevitable in any universe'

Perhaps suffering is, as philosophers would say, 'logically necessary' – inevitable in any possible world. According to Austin Farrer, natural evil is a consequence of the fact that physical objects take up space, so that matter inevitably interacts and collides with other matter. The cancer in the lung and the fungus in the foot cause pain because two things are trying to occupy the same space. 'The mutual interference of systems', Farrer claims, is 'the grand cause of physical evil'; adding that 'the physical universe could be delivered from the mutual interference of its constituent systems only by being deprived of its physicality' (Farrer, 1966, pp. 50–51). Hence God does not intend earthquakes; they are 'necessary consequences . . . of the order of Nature' (Ward, 1990, p. 52). In order to avoid such suffering, God *could* have created only minds or spirits (for example angels) that do not occupy space. But if he had restricted his creative urge in this way, God would not have created *us*.

'Suffering is a result of sin'

The 'free will defence' argues that it is better that God should have made free, responsible people who *might* do wrong, rather than not allowing free will at all. The doctrine of the Fall is an extension of this claim, and adherents of this doctrine argue that some of the natural evil in the world is a consequence of the sin of Adam or Satan (see Chapter 7).

'Suffering is necessary if the world is to be a place where we can grow up morally'

John Hick asks us to imagine a world without pain, and therefore without challenges and problems: 'life would become like a reverie in which, delightfully but aimlessly, we should float and drift at ease' (1968, p. 343). Is such a world too good to be good-for-us? Don't we want more from life, and for our children, than effortless pleasure? It is only in a world where there are real difficulties, dangers and suffering that we can develop courage and intelligence, and compassion and self-sacrifice. One of the main reasons for creating a world containing suffering is to encourage our battle against evil. To adopt John Keats' phrase, our world should be thought of as a 'vale of soul-making', and emphatically not as a harmless cage for a pampered pet. And is it not also true that it is only those who have suffered who can show us what it is like to be a real human being?

But do all 'first-order evils' give rise to these 'second-order' goods? We might respond to this criticism with an appeal to the mystery of evil, arguing that suffering has to be distributed randomly ('gratuitously') if it is to serve its soul-making function. The reason for this is that if the sufferer's pain was clearly seen to be for her ultimate good (as leading to her moral and spiritual development), or as her just desert, it would neither evoke sympathy and aid nor encourage disinterested virtue.

'Suffering paves the way to heaven'

Many argue that the soul-making begun in this world is hardly ever completed in one lifetime. This might be an argument for further moral and spiritual growth in an afterlife. Some Christians argue that the future good of heaven justifies the evil in this world, which is a necessary means to such a good end. Much of the suffering of this life might then be viewed as equivalent to the inevitable pain of childbirth, soon to be swallowed up in the joy of a new creation (remember Romans 8:18–23). However, traditional Christianity has combined this perspective with a belief in the everlasting punishment of sinners and unbelievers in hell (see Chapter 10).

EXERCISE

It is through explanations such as these that theodicy attempts to combat the claim that the existence of an all loving, all powerful God is incompatible with *the bare fact of evil* in the world. If any of these answers 'work', we cannot deduce that God does not exist from the fact that evil does. Which of these attempted solutions best fulfils this purpose?

But now ask yourself: What about the sheer quantity of suffering in God's world? Can we justify *the amount of evil and the types of evil* that innocent humans (and animals) suffer? Is there not just too much of it; and is too much of it just pointless? What do you think?

Good God?

An ancient logical problem, going back at least to the time of Plato (and discussed in his dialogue *Euthyphro*), faces anyone who attempts to argue about God's goodness. The dilemma is this: Is God good *by definition* (so that whatever God does, we have to call it good) or do *humans judge* whether God is good or not? In the first case, God might command us tomorrow to commit murder and adultery, and they would then *be* good. In the second case, we have a standard of goodness independent of God against which we judge him, a situation that compromises God's sovereignty.

Armed with a doctrine of creation, however, we may argue that our standards of judgement are themselves determined by God, at least in part, for God has made us with such a nature that we tend to call him 'good'. Is that an adequate solution (cf. Vardy, 1992, chapters 8 and 9)? And what about the more radical claim that God's 'goodness' is not actually a *moral* goodness at all? On this view, God's goodness is not like that of a person bound by duties and obligations, a goodness that can be assessed by his actions, but is to be measured rather by God's completeness of being and lack of limitation (cf. Davies, 1993, pp. 47–53). Would you argue this way?

Contrasting theodicies

According to Hick, two contrasting theodicies may be found within the Christian tradition: the 'Augustinian' and the 'Irenaean'. The chart below is constructed from his summary of their points of contrast and agreement (cf. Hick, 1968, chapter XII).

'AUGUSTINIAN'	'IRENAEAN'
(Augustine, Aquinas, Calvin, Leibniz, and many traditional and Catholic and Protestant accounts)	*(Irenaeus, Schleiermacher, Tennant, and many modern liberal accounts)*
Responsibility for evil rests on created beings (angels and/or human beings) who have misused their freedom. Moral evil is their fault, and natural evil is the inevitable consequence (punishment) for that moral evil.	It is explicitly recognised that **God is ultimately responsible for the evil in the universe.** Moral evil is the fault of free human beings that God has created and permits to sin. God has deliberately put natural evil in the world to create the best environment for soul-making.
This tradition appeals to certain metaphysical views: • evil is 'non-being' (God only creates good; evil is a going-wrong of good or is to be found where things are at the limits of existence); • while some of the parts may be ugly, the whole picture is more beautiful as a result of the contrast; • 'the principle of plenitude' (it is	*This tradition holds no such metaphysical views.*

better for God to create at all the levels of existence, so that the universe is as full as it can be of beings – including those that suffer evil or cause it).

God's relationship with the universe is impersonal. Humans are created to complete the list of types of being.

God's relationship with the universe is essentially personal. Humans are created for fellowship with God.

Looks to the past (the Fall) for an explanation of the origin of evil.

Looks to the future (heaven) for the justifying end, as God brings good out of evil.

The Fall is central to this theodicy. Adam (Man) was created perfect in a perfect world, but sinned deliberately (see Chapter 7).

The Fall is less important, or is denied altogether. Some argue that the Fall of Adam was like the sin of a child; others that mankind was created or evolved as 'fallen'. (Down here in the mud of the world, we might say, we are free to grow towards God without being overwhelmed by any direct knowledge of the divine nature.)

The present world is not how God intends it to be. It should be a paradise without suffering, and human beings need to be saved from it by God's grace.

The world is more-or-less how God intends it. It is a world with real temptations and risks: the only sort of world in which we can freely develop faith and virtue, and learn obedience through suffering, in co-operation with God's grace.

Our behaviour in this world will determine **our ultimate destination in heaven or hell.**

This tradition is **more likely to reject the notion of hell.** In the end all will be saved, perhaps through a continuing process of soul-making after death (see Chapter 10).

EXERCISE

Which of these approaches (or which parts of them) do you find most helpful in accounting for *natural evil*, and why?

Further reading

Introductory

Farrer, A (1966), *Love Almighty and Ills Unlimited*, London, Collins.

Hebblethwaite, B (1976), *Evil, Suffering and Religion*, London, Sheldon.

Hick, J (1983), *Philosophy of Religion*, Englewood Cliffs, New Jersey, Prentice-Hall, chapter 4.

Hick, J (1983), *The Second Christianity*, London, SCM, pp. 93–102.

Lewis, C S (1957), *The Problem of Pain*, London, Collins.

Pailin, D A (1992), *A Gentle Touch: from a theology of handicap to a theology of human being*, London, SPCK.

Peterson, M, Hasker, W, Reichenbach, B and Basinger, D (1991), *Reason and Religious Belief*, New York, Oxford University Press, chapter 6.

Soelle, D (1975), *Suffering*, ET London, Darton, Longman and Todd.

Vardy, P (1992), *The Puzzle of Evil*, London, HarperCollins.

Advanced

Brown, D (1989), The problem of pain, in R Morgan (ed.), *The Religion of the Incarnation: Anglican essays in commemoration of Lux Mundi*, pp. 46–59, Bristol, Bristol Classical Press.

Davies, B (1985), *Thinking about God*, London, Chapman, chapter 8.

Davies, B (1993), *An Introduction to the Philosophy of Religion*, Oxford, Oxford University Press, chapter 3.

Davis, S T (ed.) (1981), *Encountering Evil: live options in theodicy*, Edinburgh, T and T Clark.

Griffin, D (1976), *God, Power and Evil: a process theodicy*, Philadelphia, Westminster.

Hauerwas, S (1990), *Naming the Silences: God, medicine and the problem of suffering*, Grand Rapids, Michigan, Eerdmans.

Hick, J (1966, 1977, 1985), *Evil and the God of Love*, London, Macmillan.

Hick, J (1973), *God and the Universe of Faiths*, London, Macmillan, chapter 4.

Hume, D (1779), *Dialogues Concerning Natural Religion*, various editions, part X.

Moltmann, J (1974), *The Crucified God*, ET London, SCM, chapter 6.

Surin, K (1986), *Theology and the Problem of Evil*, Oxford, Blackwell.

7. SIN AND FREEDOM

Introduction

The problem of suffering covers only part of the problem of evil. Indeed, as we saw in the last chapter, many do not want to apply the language of 'evil' to suffering caused by Nature at all, preferring to restrict the word to the actions of human beings (and of any other 'moral agents' there may be) and the suffering they cause ('moral evil').

To use the term *sin* here is already to speak in theological language. Sin is defined with reference to God, as 'an offence against God' which produces alienation from God. The tabloid use of the term as shorthand for sexual immorality both secularises and absurdly limits it.

Reflecting on experience

Do you think of yourself as a sinner? In *The Book of Common Prayer* worshippers are exhorted 'to acknowledge and confess our manifold sins and wickedness'. They respond by declaring themselves 'miserable offenders' and by admitting 'there is no health in us'. Is this how you think and feel about yourself?

Thomas Cranmer, the main author of the Prayer Book and the Church of England's Articles of Religion, has been described as holding a position that 'did not view the fact of moral struggle hopefully, as a sign that God's Spirit was at work ... but gloomily, as a proof that the moral battle was lost before it was begun' (O'Donovan, 1986, p. 72). A healthy Christian spirituality should perhaps be more positive.

But even that would seem alien to many today. It is often said that the modern world has lost the 'consciousness of sin' that was so characteristic of earlier generations. Although we may be willing to acknowledge our acts of commission and omission (the wrong acts we have done and the right acts 'we have left undone'), we are less likely to view ourselves as sinners.

This resistance is partly a reaction against the strong emphasis on guilt and the negative view of human nature that Christianity has often promoted, and which the therapy and counselling professions reject as unhealthy and unhelpful for human flourishing. More theologically, we may claim that Christianity declares us saved rather than sinners, for 'Christ died for our sins' (1 Corinthians 15:3) and we now 'have been set free from sin' (Romans 6:22a).

The theology of sin

In the Bible, God's holiness and righteousness are strongly contrasted with human corruption, transgression and disobedience (this last being perhaps the 'basic sin', as in Genesis 3). The realistic psychology of the Bible recognises the inherent wickedness of the human heart (Jeremiah 17:9; Mark 7:20–23) and our vulnerability to temptation.

The Fall and original sin

The narrative in Genesis 3 describes a first sin that forfeited an ideal existence for the present hard and harsh realities of life. It does *not* imply that these were punishments to be inflicted on later generations. The story was taken up by Paul (see Romans 5:12–21), for whom all have become sinners and condemned because of one man's sin.

The doctrine of 'the Fall' of Adam, the symbol of humanity, was developed and made explicit by Augustine, who argued that the sin of our first parents deprived all human beings of their natural (in the sense of God-given) attributes of immortality and innocence (our 'original righteousness'). Three things are usually said to follow from this fall from grace:

1 we now inherit a tainted and corrupt nature and a tendency to sin ('original sin'); and
2 we also inherit personal guilt for Adam's sin ('original guilt') as well as
3 suffering the natural evil of pain, suffering and death as a proper punishment for the Fall.

For Augustine, all this is explained in terms of the 'seminal identity' of the whole human race in Adam's loins (an updated version might talk about our 'presence' in his DNA coding). Augustine writes:

God created man aright, for God is the author of natures, though he is certainly not responsible for their defects. But man was willingly perverted and justly condemned, and so begot perverted and condemned offspring. For we were all in that one man, seeing that we all were that one man who fell into sin through the woman who was made from him before the first sin. (Augustine, 1972, p. 523)

In Augustine's thinking, then, we are all born soiled and condemned as part of our 'genetic endowment'.

EXERCISE

Although profoundly influential in the history of Christian theology, the concept of original sin has been condemned even by those (like Immanuel Kant) who recognise in human beings a radical inclination to evil. 'Pelagianism', named after the British lay theologian who took on Augustine himself in the fifth century, rejected the view that original sin is an inherited defect impairing our freedom to do good. Augustine's account has been described as the 'astonishing doctrine of innate and biologically inherited sin and guilt' (Quinn, 1997, p. 544).

Why do you think that the doctrine has been so widely criticised?

Perhaps the protests are understandable. It is difficult to see how Augustine's view can withstand the moral objections brought against it, to which we must now add scientific evidence about human origins. In particular, we may note the difficulty of affirming:
• that there ever was a sinless, deathless paradise on earth;
• that there ever was a unique individual, an historical Adam, the ancestor of the whole human race; and, especially,
• that it is right for a child to suffer for the sins of its father. This view is rejected, of course, in the Bible itself (see Deuteronomy 24:16 and Ezekiel 18; although it is endorsed in Exodus 20:5 and elsewhere).

Even if Adam existed, it would be difficult to accept that his sin and guilt was in any way *our* sin and guilt, whether as a result of corporate solidarity or genetic inheritance, or because Adam is our representative in a covenant with God (as in Calvin's theology). I cannot perform another's act; and surely I can only be guilty of my own acts?

EXERCISE

Despite these comments, do you find any value in the Augustinian doctrine of original sin? Can it be salvaged?

You might argue that it chimes in with our experience of the habitual, social and universal character of human sinfulness. Some would wish to follow F R Tennant in finding a 'genetic explanation' of our tendency to sin not in any inherited sinfulness of the mind, but simply in our 'non-moral and necessary animal instinct and self-assertive tendency', honed through the forces of evolution (Tennant, 1906, p. 11; cf. Williams, 1927, pp. 169–170, who identifies it with our 'herd instinct'). These habits and tendencies were originally useful and not sinful; now they are anachronisms that work against our moral development.

Keith Ward develops this emphasis on our evolved biological drives (to 'sexuality', 'territorial possession' and 'aggression') in a social direction, to show how the whole human world has become trapped in egoism. He argues that a society marked by 'greed, hatred, and delusion' was created by an early universal rejection of God by humans, as they let their natural drives of desire and self-regard have their head (Ward, 1998, chapter 8). We may still wish to think of this as a sort of 'fall'.

Sex and salvation?

Augustine held that human desire ('concupiscence'), particularly unbridled sexual desire, is another result of the Fall. It is not itself sin but it corrupts our love of things and people; original sin continues to be transmitted down the generations through it. In the Augustinian tradition, original sin is only dealt with (along with our own actual sins) by the cleansing power of Christian baptism. For Augustine, although baptism washes away all our sins it does not take away the infirmity of desire, so we must continue to fight against this incentive to sin. For Calvin, this desire itself was truly a sin, but its guilt is abolished through Christ's saving power. In traditional Catholic theology, baptised Christians may still be separated from God by committing a 'mortal sin'. Without the Church's forgiveness through the sacrament of reconciliation or penance, the sinner would then receive eternal damnation. Less heinous 'venial sins' do not risk such alienation from God.

Protestant theology tends to reject this distinction among sins and to identify the cure for sin solely in God's forgiving love, which reorientates the sinner's life, rather than focusing on the sinner's acts of penance or the ministrations of the Church. The sin of the saved Christian is no longer 'counted against' him by God. Luther's early view that we are sinners in ourselves yet righteous in God's eyes ('at the same time both a sinner and righteous') emphasises *both* our worthlessness and rejection (in and of ourselves, in our sin and faithlessness) *and* our wholeness and acceptance (in God's faithfulness, promise and salvation).

Image breaking?

The Fall is seen by some Christians as a total loss of true virtue, our knowledge of God and our freedom. It is sometimes argued that after the Fall the only freedom left to humans without God's grace is the 'freedom to sin'. This view, which was sternly held by both Luther and Calvin, and is expressed more moderately in the Thirty-Nine Articles (see articles 9, 10 and 13), has been much modified in recent liberal Protestant theology. Catholic teaching was always more resistant to the belief that 'total depravity' is a consequence of the Fall, and allows for a continuing (though weak and debased) human freedom.

Another way of putting this disagreement is in terms of the doctrine of the 'image of God' (*imago dei*), in which God created men and women (Genesis 1:26–27). For many of the Protestant Reformers, this image was either completely effaced at the Fall or so corrupted that all that remains is 'but horrible deformity', a 'blunted relic' of the image of God. But for Aquinas and most Catholics, God's image (understood here primarily as reason – including religious and moral reason) remains intact in the sinner, with only the 'likeness to God' being destroyed at the Fall. The Eastern Orthodox Churches never embraced Augustine's theology, and consider that the only loss of the Fall is the loss of righteousness or holiness. This is more a matter of weakness deserving divine compassion, than an offence meriting God's wrath.

In theological debate on this topic, the image of God sometimes refers to specific human attributes, such as our freedom or wisdom, and sometimes to a spiritual or supernatural feature – our fundamental orientation to and relationship with God. Two different analogies are being employed here.

• On the one hand, 'the *imago* may be thought of as an image, such as Caesar's, which is stamped on a coin.' On this analogy, the image would be sought in some human faculties such that if our image were obliterated, we would no longer be human, let alone a sinner.

- 'On the other hand, the *imago* may be thought of as the image that is reflected in a mirror. Although the mirror remains a mirror, it no longer reflects our image if we do not stand in front of it.' According to this second analogy, the image of God is a matter of relationship, and will be completely lost if we no longer reflect God in our life (Hordern, 1969b, p. 203).

Sin and theodicy

EXERCISE

Look again at the chart in the previous chapter that contrasts the 'Augustinian' and 'Irenaean' theodicies, noting particularly their understanding of the Fall and God's intention for his world. Which of these alternatives offers the better assessment of the place of *human sin* in God's world?

Although Irenaeus also acknowledges a Fall that is the fault of Man and not of God, he argues that all creatures are imperfect and lack discipline and knowledge. On this account evil is rooted in the nature of created existence itself; for Irenaeus our world is one 'in which the occurrence of error and sin is not merely possible but probable' (Norris, 1966, p. 77). But God can remedy this human condition, and we may trust that God will do so by strengthening and perfecting human nature through the processes of history.

But is Irenaeus too soft on sin: another example, perhaps, of too much understanding and not enough condemnation? This chapter has been rather scathing about Augustinian theology, perhaps unjustly. You may argue that at least it captures the seriousness of sin, and is realistic about the dire consequences of rebellion against God.

The free will defence
In this traditional 'solution' to the problem of moral evil, sin is taken very seriously indeed. The argument goes like this. It is better that God should have created free responsible beings who might do wrong rather than puppets, robots or automata that could never do wrong. Moral evil is the risk God takes in creating beings with free will.

The free will defence has been applied both to humans and to angelic powers. In this second application the claim is that there was a

Fall of angels, perhaps before the creation of the physical world, which resulted in powerful spiritual sources of natural evil and temptation existing over against God. By contrast with one of the 'easy answers' offered in Chapter 6, this is only a *penultimate* dualism. There are not two gods; even Satan is a created being who can be destroyed. But God is responsible for giving Satan freedom and for allowing him to continue to exist after his rebellion, although Satan alone is responsible for his own sin. As belief in the existence of Satan declines this becomes a less popular defence, but some Christians argue that it is perfectly reasonable 'to maintain that the free will of heavenly beings . . . limits God's power' in this way (Vardy, 1992, p. 180).

In its application to the sin of Adam or (more usually today) to some less specific ancestral fall of the whole human species, the free will defence is also often extended to explain *natural evil* as a punishment for the sin of the Fall and for our own actual sins. While there are biblical passages that endorse the claim that human suffering arises as the appropriate punishment for sin, and health and happiness is bestowed as a fitting reward for obedience, other texts present quite the opposite view:

📖 **Read Deuteronomy 7:12–16 and 28:1–24; Job 8 and 15:17–35; Psalms 37 and 39; Acts 5:1–11; *contrast* Deuteronomy 24:16; Job 21; Psalm 73:1–14 (but cf. verses 16–28); John 9:1–3; cf. Luke 13:1–5.**

Hints in the Bible of a 'Fall of Nature' (Genesis 3:14–19; Romans 8:20) offer a different perspective on natural evil.

There is another way in which the free will defence may help to explain part of the problem of suffering. Only by knowing natural evil and how it is produced and avoided can we properly exercise our responsibility to prevent it. Further, the more suffering there is in the world, the more opportunities for virtue there are (cf. Swinburne, 1979, pp. 214–215). Certainly, suffering has got to be *possible* for virtue to be exercised. I can only make you well or happy if it is possible for you to be sick and miserable; helping you is only a virtue in a world where my actions could do you harm. 'In a situation in which no one can ever suffer injury or be liable to pain or suffering there would be no distinction between right and wrong action' (Hick, 1981, p. 47).

We may also note that there must be a regularity about the order of Nature, or else we would not be able to predict the effects of our own free actions. But this regularity itself often produces suffering (see Chapter 6).

EXERCISE

The most common use of the free will defence is in its application to the wrongdoing of individual human beings. It is employed here to absolve God from blame for our sinful acts, and for those of Hitler, Stalin and Saddam Hussein. This seems reasonable enough, for how can I blame God for what I have freely done?

But is the value of freedom so great that it can justify any misuse? Is this a reasonable defence?

Many think so, and perhaps you agree. But then, are we really free?

What price freedom?

If the burden of responsibility for my wrongdoing is to fall on me rather than on God, I must possess some real freedom of action over against God. But does not the doctrine of creation imply the opposite? Antony Flew writes, 'As Creator [God] must be first cause, prime mover, supporter and controller of every thought and action throughout his utterly dependent universe. In short: if creation is in, autonomy is out' (Flew, 1966, p. 47).

Theology rejects the inference: 'If God's power is understood as the expression of his love . . . then God's power is his power to give independence, autonomy, even to creatures over whom, strictly speaking, he is sovereign' (Jantzen, 1984, p. 152). To avoid a scenario in which God is totally responsible for all our actions, there must be some sort of 'gap' between God's activity and our own. On such an account, although we have freedom to act against God's will, we are still dependent on God's sustaining power for our continued being (and therefore, in one sense, for our actions).

Most theologians recognise that the free will defence can only apply to agents whose choices are not fully determined by other causes. On this definition of freedom of the will, it would not be logically possible to create free agents whose choices always go one way rather than another, and so not logically possible to create free human agents who necessarily would commit no sin (Swinburne, 1977a, p. 86).

Such a freedom would be incompatible with the claim of 'determinism' (sometimes called 'hard determinism'), which is the assertion that every event in the universe is causally determined by previous events or (more precisely) that 'in the case of everything that exists, there are antecedent conditions, known or unknown, given which that thing could not be other than it is' (Taylor, 1963, p. 34). This is a wide-ranging, metaphysical claim. Many scientists argue that it has now been disproved, for there do seem to be subatomic events (for example the movements of electrons) that are not completely determined by an earlier state of affairs. But we have seen (in Chapter 5) that freedom of the will involves much more than that. It requires that our behaviour should sometimes be self-determined, not undetermined – 'self-caused', not 'uncaused'.

But can we defend this 'strong view' of human freedom? We must respond first to the arguments of 'soft determinists', for whom freedom means much less than this. They follow Hume in claiming that to be free is simply to be free of external constraints, like a prisoner released from jail. We could be said to be free in *this* sense even if our choosing and acting is in principle completely predictable because it is completely determined, and we could not have decided or acted any differently. But our behaviour would be free only in the sense that it was externally unconstrained.

EXERCISE

On this analysis of freedom the free will defence fails, in that God *could* then have created 'free' people who are guaranteed always to do the right thing (Flew, 1955; Mackie, 1971 and 1984, pp. 162–176). God would only need to give them the correct sort of good character, which they would then express in right actions.

How would you reply to this argument?

Persons or puppets?

Is one consideration that the freedom at issue here is our freedom in relation to God? John Gaskin writes: 'I would not be morally accountable to God if he had not freely allowed me to be an agent, able, sometimes, to choose without physical necessitation, and therefore able to do things which God did not know about in advance' (Gaskin, 1984, p. 133).

Most of us would agree that we are only *responsible* for our choices if they are free in this more radical sense. As God could only hold us responsible under these circumstances, God must have given us some sort of *real freedom*. As Hick suggests, the 'freedom' from external constraint possessed by Flew and Mackie's consistent saints would be like the 'freedom' of patients acting out a series of posthypnotic suggestions:

> they appear to themselves to be free, but their volitions have actually been predetermined by the will of the hypnotist, in relation to whom the patients are therefore not genuinely free agents ... while God *could* have created such beings, there would have been no point in doing so – at least not if God is seeking to create sons and daughters rather than human puppets. (Hick, 1983a, p. 42)

Quite. The free will defence requires the stronger view of freedom that we outlined earlier. This is freedom as limited creativity: 'inner freedom' or 'self-determined' activity. Such (partly) self-caused actions are truly *creative* activities. We are not just responding to, or acting as channels for, influences from outside ourselves; we are really doing something new. Philip Hefner describes humans as 'created co-creators' with God, and argues that it is in this capacity that we may discover 'our likeness to God and our origin and destiny in God' (Hefner, 1984, p. 327).

But our decisions and actions are always *also* partly controlled and determined by factors over which we have no say. Our freedom can only be a limited freedom; we are never wholly free. Our behaviour is the result of our decisions and actions *and* our genes, environment and the chemistry of our brains. Yet on occasions we certainly feel ourselves to be the significant, responsible, originating causes of our own behaviour, doing things that cannot just be explained by preceding conditions or causes. These are *our* decisions and acts, we insist. We feel that we do them 'on our own'.

This is perhaps best revealed in situations of moral effort, where I know myself to be free to do x *or* y, despite the forces, urges and temptations to which I am subject. Think what it is like to get out of bed on a cold, dark morning. Many factors constrain us to stay in bed, but most days we exercise our freedom and 'by an effort of the will' make our own decision and perform our own action by crawling out from under the duvet. If getting up ever becomes a morally momentous act, that taste of freedom may be even stronger. Belief in the freedom of the will must appeal, in the end, to this sort of experience.

Of course, this feeling of freedom *may* be an illusion. But many would claim that unless we have some real freedom, our existence is pointless. What do you think?

Further reading

Introductory

Baker, J A (1970), *The Foolishness of God*, London, Collins, chapters 3 to 6.

Cowburn, J (1979), *Shadows and the Dark: the problems of suffering and evil*, London, SCM.

Young, N (1976), *Creator, Creation and Faith*, London, Collins, chapter 3.

Westermann, C (1971), *Creation*, ET London, SPCK, chapter 4.

Advanced

Cairns, D (1973), *The Image of God in Man*, London, Collins.

Farrer, A (1958), *The Freedom of the Will*, London, A and C Black.

Gunton, C E (ed.) (1995), *God and Freedom: essays in historical and systematic theology*, Edinburgh, T and T Clark.

Lucas, J R (1976), *Freedom and Grace*, London, SPCK, chapters 1 and 6.

Mackie, J L (1982), *The Miracle of Theism: arguments for and against the existence of God*, Oxford, Clarendon, chapter 9.

Midgley, M (1980), *Beast and Man: the roots of human nature*, London, Methuen.

Midgley, M (1986), *Wickedness: a philosophical essay*, London, Routledge and Kegan Paul.

Schoonenberg, P (1965), *Man and Sin: a theological view*, ET London, Sheed and Ward.

Swinburne, R (1989), *Responsibility and Atonement*, Oxford, Clarendon.

Ward, K (1998), *Religion and Human Nature*, Oxford, Clarendon, chapter 8.

(See also the further reading for Chapter 6.)

8. NATURE IN GOD, GOD IN NATURE?

Introduction

At times Nature seems so solid, so stable, so *substantial*. Think of a mountain and the great age of its rocks, the vast 'unquenchable sea' or the fixed stars ('I am constant as the northern star', boasted Shakespeare's Julius Caesar).

But at other times all seems to be flux and *change*: the brief life of the mayfly; the ceaseless movement of the world's waters (Heraclitus asserted that you cannot step into the same river twice); the change, development or evolution of living organisms and eroding landscapes, even of drifting continents and exploding supernovae.

This changeableness seems to be closer to the truth about Nature. But how do you feel about it, and how do these reflections impinge on your view of God?

Reflecting on experience
In a world of change, where is God to be found? And what sort of a God is this?

For many, God is the one 'who changest not', though 'change and decay' and 'earth's vain shadows' are seen all around (see the hymn 'Abide with me'). God is the solid Rock amid the shifting sand (see Psalm 62): not only constant in character and intention ('I the LORD do not change', Malachi 3:6 NRSV), but unchanging in his very being.

The 'classical' God

Once the philosophers really got their hands on the biblical concept of God, particularly under the influence of the work of Aristotle, the concept was refined to produce a consistent account of just such a kind.

So called 'classical theism', as expounded by Thomas Aquinas and his intellectual successors ('Thomists'), describes God as an 'immutable' (unchanging) substance, utterly distinct from and independent of the world of space, time and change. Indeed, Thomas' full-blown account defines God as *pure act* without any unrealised potentialities. It also says that, although the creation has a real relation to God, in God there is no real relation to creatures. (See Mascall, 1945; Owen, 1971, chapter 1; Gilson, 1994.)

Without going all the way with this analysis, many Christians still want to defend the doctrines of God's immutability and timeless existence. Even the idea of God as 'impassible' ('without passions', not liable to suffering) has its supporters, at least to the extent of saying that God is emotionally 'touched' but not emotionally 'crushed' by what goes on in the world (Creel, 1997, p. 318).

EXERCISE

How satisfactory do you find this 'classical' analysis of the nature of God, both theologically and spiritually?

You will not be alone if you think that the account is rather problematic. Many theologians reject it as incompatible with the biblical picture of a living, responsive and loving God. According to David Pailin, it is suitable only for 'a static, self-centred, only self-knowing absolute' (1989, p. 33).

Process philosophy

The classical account of God and God's relation to the world has been particularly severely criticised by 'process thinkers', whose metaphysical debt is to Alfred North Whitehead. In *Process and Reality* and other works, Whitehead offered a view of Nature that he believed was more scientific than the received account of independent, discrete things.

According to process philosophy, this is how reality should be analysed:

- The world is a process of change.
- Time is an essential aspect of all reality.
- The ultimate constituents of the cosmos are events ('actual entities' or 'actual occasions'), not substances (things). Actual entities are individual moments of experience, 'droplets of becoming'. 'Enduring entities' are made up of these occasions, functioning as unified wholes.
- The world is an interdependent and interrelated organic whole: a community of events, with all its parts relating to ('prehending' or 'feeling' – a sort of non-sensory perception) all other parts.
- There is freedom and unpredictability throughout the universe. All events are unique centres of spontaneity and self-creation, influenced by and responding to all other events.
- All events are dipolar, with a 'mental pole' of possibility (aim) that grasps ideas and values and a 'physical pole' of actuality (becoming) that prehends or takes account of its own past, all other entities and God's leading intention for it.
- All events have worth or significance in themselves, in contributing to future events in Nature or in contributing to God; every achievement of value is taken up into God's life.
- Persuasion is more effective than coercion; God influences the world by his love, without determining it or controlling it by his power.

The key categories for this view of reality are 'process', 'becoming', 'change', 'event' and 'motion'. This sets it radically apart from classical theology's emphasis on 'substance', 'being', 'essence' and 'rest'.

Process theology

EXERCISE
Pause at this point and consider what the nature of God might be like on a process view.

The essential claim of process theology is that God is not the supreme exception but the 'chief exemplification' of these principles. Schubert Ogden writes that God is 'the unique or in all ways perfect instance of creative becoming . . . the one reality which is eminently social and temporal' (Ogden, 1977, p. 59). Everything changes – and that includes God.

For Whitehead, God is dipolar too. God's nature may therefore be analysed into (a) an *antecedent* or *primordial* ('eternal', 'absolute') aspect, and (b) a *consequent* ('temporal' – though 'everlasting' – and 'relative') aspect. Whitehead describes God's primordial nature as 'conceptual', suggesting an abstract concept. But others distinguish it as God's 'mental pole', his 'timeless envisagement of possibilities' which is 'eternally unchanging' (Cobb, 1966, p. 155) but which lures the world forward to realise novel possibilities. God's consequent nature is described by Whitehead as 'conscious' and by John Cobb as 'God's physical pole, his prehension of the actual occasions constituting the temporal world' (pp. 161–162). In this latter respect, God is affected by and (partly) caused by the world, absorbing its effects so that all things achieve an 'objective immortality' in God's consequent being. Thus, unlike the God of 'monopolar' classical theism, the Process God is supremely *responsive* to the world. (We may compare the distinction made in Eastern Orthodox theology between God's *essence*, as transcendent incomprehensible mystery, and God's *energies*, in the sense of his activity directed towards the universe – creating, enlivening and caring for all creatures.)

For Charles Hartshorne this *dipolar theism* is expressed differently, for God (who is pictured as a society of entities) is analysed in terms of (a) the mere abstraction of God's 'abstract essence': independent, necessary existence, eternal and immutable; and (b) God's 'consequent states': the concrete 'exemplification' of divine existence in a God who is personal and in process, changing, contingent and relative. This latter pole is the actual God: 'God as consequent upon the world' (Griffin, 1992, p. 386).

God in process?

God is therefore a changing *process* that transcends, but includes, the perishing events of the spatio-temporal world. God's experiences change in so far as God receives from the world and contributes to it; God experiences all that happens. 'The love of the world passes into the love of heaven, and floods back into the world. In this sense, God is the great companion – the fellow-sufferer who understands' (Whitehead, 1967, p. 532). All entities are therefore co-creators of God's consequent nature. And for process theology, our life after death may be seen in terms of the 'objective immortality' that all things have, cherished everlastingly in God's conscious consequent nature.

But God acts as well as being acted upon. God too is co-creator of all that he influences. God is also the ground of all novelty: 'Apart from God there would be nothing new in the world' (Whitehead, 1967, p. 377). But God can only persuade ('lure') not coerce; and since actual entities are partly self-determining, the free will defence will apply to all events and natural evil can be explained in this way.

You are probably already thinking that this account is no clearer than that offered by Aquinas! Theologians of both traditions have a right to respond to such a complaint, however, by pointing out that science's description of the humble atom is exceedingly complicated and difficult to grasp. Do we really expect the nature of God to be simpler than that?

In any case, the basic theme of process theology is straightforward. God is actually *relative*, rather than *absolute*, changing through sympathetic participation in the world. God is genuinely related to the world, so human actions can make a difference to God. God will always exist and is perfect in love; but God is not totally sovereign over Nature, which has its own freedom.

God in contrast

The main differences between classical and process (or 'neo-classical') theology can be summed up under two headings (cf. Pittenger, 1969, p. 37).

God's infinite nature

(See Ward, 1982, chapter 10.) For classical theism, God is 'exclusively infinite': not limited by anything other than himself. For process theology, God is 'inclusively infinite': there is nothing 'outside' God to limit God, for all things are 'in' God.

On the former view, God excludes the finite world and God's perfection lies in his difference from it, untainted by imperfection. The world can add nothing to God. On the latter view, God is 'perfect-perfectible' and 'finite-infinite' (Hartshorne); nothing can surpass God, but God can surpass himself. God *includes* all that is finite. While God's love and knowledge do not increase as God 'grows', the objects of God's love and knowledge do change and increase, and so the divine experience is enriched and changes. But God (abstractly) always knows all that is to be known, and loves perfectly all there is to be loved; it is 'God's concrete states' that exemplify this 'relative type of perfection, a perfection that can be surpassed' (Griffin, 1992, p. 386).

God's relation to the world

(See Chapter 1 above.) For classical theism, the world is related to (because dependent on) God, but God is not really related to the world. God is independent of the world and completely different from it (transcendent). Some claim that the world can make no difference to a God who is impassible and immutable. In process theology, by contrast, everything is in flux, and a changing God is intimately associated with a changing Nature. The world affects God and is truly related to God. God's creative power is to be found essentially in God's influence within the universe – bringing order out of chaos and actualising potentialities.

No entity comes into existence without God. According to Whitehead, God does not actually create the universe out of nothing and there never was a beginning of the world. Things create themselves; God simply gives to each actual occasion its initial aim. Yet continuous creation may form a part of process thought, for the world can be seen as dependent on God for its existence as well as supremely influenced by God. And Cobb argues that 'to a greater degree than Whitehead intended, God must be conceived as being the reason that entities occur at all as well as determining the limits within which they can achieve their own forms' (Cobb, 1966, p. 211).

EXERCISE

Re-read the two sections above, trying to get clear about the differences between the 'classical' and 'process' pictures of God and the world.

Should Christian theology prefer the process view?

In many ways process theology does seem to be closer to the biblical picture of God than does classical theism. And it is certainly difficult to explain or defend the idea of God as immutable, pure act, timeless, etc. However, process thought involves a considerable amount of speculation and commits us to a rather odd view of the universe, in which our human experience of ourselves and events in process are taken as the appropriate models for understanding *all* reality. This results from Whitehead's 'reformed subjectivist principle', which is his claim that our knowledge of God and the universe must be based on what we know as subjects of our own experience, as changing *selves*. The world and its

God are like us, then: all 'process' and 'creative becoming', not 'substance' or 'being' (cf. Ogden, 1977, chapter I).

Colin Gunton charges process theology with replacing personal language about God's love, mercy and grace with impersonal notions such as 'relation' that apply to all entities and are not dependent on the exercise of any voluntary choice. He also scolds process thinkers for their doctrine of a finite God: 'it is of little benefit to overthrow a tyrant if he is replaced by an ineffectual weakling.' In process theology, Gunton argues, God is in part created *after* things in the world have ceased to be; they create God, rather than the other way around! Finally, he accuses process theology of being no more than a highly mythological, 'sophisticated form of animism' which, in divinising the world, 'represents a superstitious form of idolatry' (Gunton, 1978, p. 223).

What do you think?

God and world revisited

For process theology the universe exists in God. It is thus a *panentheistic* view: 'God includes the world but is more than the world' (Hartshorne, 1976, p. 90). God needs his body, the world, and yet: 'To be himself he does not need *this* universe but only *a* universe . . . The mere essence of God contains no universe. We are truly 'outside' the divine essence, though inside God' (Hartshorne and Reese, 1953, p. 22).

As we saw back in Chapter 1, such a view has both strengths and weaknesses. It appears in a different, and rather more *pantheistic*, guise in the more radical spiritualities of Nature which we consider next.

The earth as Gaia

The British scientist James Lovelock (an agnostic) developed the 'Gaia hypothesis' in the 1970s, adopting the name of the Greek goddess of the earth to label a view that this planet is a self-regulating system, operating almost like a living organism. He argued that biological life affects the physical and chemical conditions of the life-supporting atmosphere, oceans and land masses in a way that keeps them constant, at exactly the right quantity and proportions for life to flourish (although he insists that this feedback is not specifically for *human* survival). For Lovelock this is an automatic feedback process, not the product of some 'earthmind'. He does not say that the earth *is* a living organism, only that it behaves *like* an organism.

Others have not been as cautious. Lovelock's basic theme has been taken up and enthusiastically developed by 'New Age' spirituality, as well as by popular 'Green' movements. All of them welcome the recognition of our interdependent connectedness with Nature. Some think of Gaia as conscious and advocate communication ('conversation') with it.

Many 'ecofeminists' find the tradition of biblical and Christian spirituality oppressive and look to alternative, often naturalistic spiritualities for strength and sustenance in their projects and values. For them, the universe is itself a divine process bringing redemption. They reject any attitude to life that understands Nature (which is often spoken of as feminine) as seeking to be dominated, and implies that women should serve men as Nature serves culture and that animals exist only for the service of the human race.

EXERCISE

What do you make of these different types of 'Gaia thinking'?

What, if anything, can Christians learn from them?

Gaia language encourages a sense of the integrity of creation that is greatly needed. It helps us resist separative, 'parts-only' thinking about Nature. The idea of a whole 'web' or 'system' of interdependent created beings – at least on this planet – is valuable. Some Christians have therefore been sympathetic to Gaia thinking.

But others warn of the danger of replacing the biblical emphasis on encounter with a transcendent God with a spirituality of oneness with Nature. Critics argue that, although the earth is a system that supports life and is to some extent self-regulating, there is no evidence for calling the whole system 'alive' or 'conscious'. There are dangers too in supposing that the earth's self-regulatory systems will *always* manage to sustain life, whatever harm we do to our planet. And Nature also has her malevolent side. To those who value human life, the mindless, amoral forces of Nature may appear to be rather less than they had hoped for in a God.

Many Christians insist that a spirituality of pantheism (or 'Naturism') will lead to a subjugation of the human and personal in favour of some impersonal 'balance of Nature'. For some 'deep ecologists', humans are less important than their environment and may be viewed as something like a plague weed or cancerous growth upon the earth, essentially harmful to Gaia. Even for Lovelock, 'we are just another species, neither the owners nor the stewards of this planet' (Lovelock, 1988, p. 14). Many are concerned by the implications of this perspective for our view of the status and character of human beings.

But we might still argue that Gaia-talk evokes a sense of the importance of Nature and is therefore a valuable counterbalance to our human (or is it just male?) temptation to exploit it.

Oppression or stewardship?

In the first chapter of Genesis, which is the *later* of the two great creation stories in the Bible, human beings are told to 'subdue' the earth (Genesis 1:26–28) and are given power over the animals. Many ecologically-sensitive readers feel uneasy with this sort of language; some have argued that it has served as a divine licence for human exploitation of the rest of creation for far too long. The historian Lynn White contends that this God-given mandate to exercise dominion has resulted in our present ecological crisis. It is a crisis for which Christianity must bear a 'huge burden of guilt' (White, 1967, p. 81).

EXERCISE

📖 Re-read the two stories of creation in Genesis 1:1 to 2:4a and 2:4b–25.

Is White's criticism of the theology of Nature in Genesis fair?

Note that in the *earlier* creation narrative of Genesis 2, the man ('Adam') is put in the Garden of Eden 'to cultivate and guard it' (Genesis 2:15). Although his naming of the animals in this narrative (2:19) shows humanity's dominion over them, the context suggests that the beasts are offered as possible 'suitable companions' for the man (like him they are created from the soil) before the woman is created as a proper complement and completion of human creation. The essential theme is that humanity is to be God's gardener and obedient agent *caring* for the creation (cf. Deuteronomy 22:6–7; Leviticus 25:1–7). So here the proper model of our relationship to Nature is that of 'stewardship' and responsibility, accompanied by a sense of respect for and kinship with the rest of creation, rather than greedy exploitation and rapacious asset-stripping.

Christians should interpret human dominion over Nature in the same way as they understand the sovereignty of a God who exercises his divinity by laying aside power and becoming the caring servant, respecting rather than dominating his creatures (cf. Philippians 2:5–11; Mark 10:42–45). Many theologians argue further for a relationship between humanity and the rest of creation that is modelled on the mutuality and community that exists within the Trinity. Speaking solely of God as Father may give the wrong message about God's relationship with creation (as autocratic, domineering, powerful, patriarchal and impassible), unless it is properly explained and qualified. The divine activity might be viewed very differently if God is also described as Spirit, and understood as an immanent presence indwelling creation and bringing it to its appointed goal (and often described in more feminine and maternal language). The same may be said of God understood as God the Son, or God as Word, acting cosmically as the agent of creation but revealed most fully in the caring, non-violent, healing and rescuing figure of Jesus Christ (see Chapter 10).

Ecological values

The doctrine of creation, properly interpreted, should generate an ecological ethic expressing our duty of care for the world. Science, as well as religion, has a shameful past here. The picture of a mechanistic and totally determined universe, as portrayed by earlier scientific thinking, often led to a brutal attitude towards the world. Today's more open, emergent and hierarchical portrait of Nature is likely to be rather more tender. Evolutionary biology has blurred the distinction between humans and the rest of Nature, and the sciences of animal and plant ecology have uncovered the interconnectedness and vulnerability of life on earth. This may lead to what Peter Hodgson has described as an 'ecological cosmology' (Hodgson, 1994, p. 92).

But there is no guarantee that the study of science alone will generate environmental values. Religion *should* be able to help here. Process theology, sacramental theology, radically immanentist creation-spirituality, and a whole spectrum of other forms of Christian theology, can effectively engender a deep respect for Nature. God does not have to be seen as 'the enemy of Nature' or 'the owner of Nature'. It is also possible to adopt the metaphors of Nature's 'redeemer', 'husband' and 'internal spirit' (McFague, 1993; cf. Comstock, 1997).

How do *you* think of God's relationship to Nature?

Further reading on process theology

Introductory

Cobb, J B and Griffin, D R (1977), *Process Theology: an introductory exposition*, Belfast, Christian Journals.

Fiddes, P S (1993), Process theology, in A E McGrath (ed.), *The Blackwell Encyclopedia of Modern Christian Thought*, pp. 472–476, Oxford, Blackwell.

Pailin, D A (1986), *Groundwork of Philosophy of Religion*, London, Epworth, chapters 6 and 7.

Surin, K, (1989), Process theology, in D Ford (ed.), *The Modern Theologians, Vol. II*, pp. 103–114, Oxford, Blackwell.

Advanced

Brown, D, James, R E and Reeves, G (eds) (1971), *Process Philosophy and Christian Thought*, Indianapolis, Indiana, Bobbs-Merrill.

Cobb, J B (1966), *A Christian Natural Theology: based on the thought of Alfred North Whitehead*, London, Lutterworth.

Pailin, D A (1989), *God and the Processes of Reality: foundations of a credible theism*, London, Routledge.

Further reading on Gaia and the theology of Nature

Introductory

Astley, J and Day, D (1996), *Beyond the Here and Now*, Oxford, Lion, chapters 1, 2, 3, 5, 7.

Deane-Drummond, C (1996), *A Handbook in Theology and Ecologys*, London, SCM.

Fox, M (1991), *Creation Spirituality*, San Francisco, HarperSanFrancisco.

Poole, M (1995), *Beliefs and Values in Science Education*, Buckingham, Open University Press, chapter 4.

Advanced

Clark, S R L (1993), *How to Think about the Earth: philosophical and theological models for ecology*, London, Mowbray.

Deane-Drummond, C (1996), *A Handbook in Theology and Ecology*, London, SCM.

Hodgson, P C (1994), *Winds of the Spirit: a constructive Christian theology*, London, SCM, chapter 7.

McFague, S (1987), *Models of God: theology for an ecological, nuclear age*, London, SCM, especially chapter 3.

Moltmann, J (1985), *God in Creation: an ecological doctrine of creation*, ET London, SCM.

Page, R (1996), *God and the Web of Creation*, London, SCM.

Ruether, R R (1992), *Gaia and God: an ecofeminist theology of earth healing*, London, SCM.

Russell, C A (1994), *The Earth, Humanity and God*, London, UCL Press.

9. LIFE AFTER DEATH

Introduction

Most people would say that religion has two basic beliefs: the existence of God and life after death. Opinion polls show that only just over 30% of the general population of mainland Britain believe that a personal God exists. (Although around 67% say that they 'believe in God', the majority of them mean by 'God' an impersonal force or power.) By contrast, belief in life after death is affirmed by about 49% of the population. Among weekly church-goers, belief in a life after death rises to 83%, which is very close to the figure in this group for belief in a personal God (Gill, 1999, pp. 70, 128).

Reflecting on experience

How important is a belief in life after death to you? In your experience, how central is it to the faith of other Christians?

Many would follow Saint Paul in claiming that 'if our hope in Christ is good for this life only and no more, then we deserve more pity than anyone else in all the world' (1 Corinthians 15:19 GNB). Others are more agnostic and perhaps even dismissive of a faith that focuses too closely on 'pie in the sky when you die'.

Grounds for hope: revelation

EXERCISE
📖 Read Psalms 30:8–10 and 88:10–13; Job 10:21–22; Isaiah 38:16–19. Afterwards read Psalm 139:1–12.

What sort of 'future hope' is presented here?

It is an arresting fact that for most of the Old Testament period belief in a life after death was either absent or, if present, was treated as a peripheral belief in which one could invest little hope. For Israelite religion, 'life' meant this life. It was 'now' that one had a relationship with God, 'here' was where one could serve God and be blessed by God. Any afterlife was no more than a gloomy, perhaps unconscious, half-existence in *Sheol* ('The Pit'), a subterranean place from which God was absent and darkness reigned. Today, the radical ('non-realist') Christian theologian Don Cupitt embraces an even more stark, this-worldly, disinterested spirituality that allows no room for a future hope (Cupitt, 1980, 1992; cf. Phillips, 1970).

Other cultures held firm beliefs in life after death from an early period (recall the Egyptian pyramids) and it may be that influences from Zoroastrian religion pushed Israelite theology towards a fuller hope during the time of the Exile in Babylonia in the sixth century BC. The affirmation in Psalm 139:8 that the psalmist will not be cut off from God's presence even in the world of the dead marks a theological break-through.

But we find only the beginnings of a belief that God will raise the dead in very late texts (Daniel 12:1–3; Isaiah 26:19; and possibly Job 19:23–27). Three convictions might have contributed to this developing hope:

• God is supreme in love and power. Since God creates us and values our lives, God will not allow that value to fall out of existence.
• We die incomplete and unfinished, having only begun to walk the road towards spiritual and moral maturity. God will surely allow us to continue that development, which he so desires and for which we have been created.
• In this world the righteous suffer more than they ought, as Job found. A God of justice will want to restore some sort of 'moral balance' in

another life. Interestingly, the context of the resurrection texts in the Old Testament is often that of blatant injustice. The claim is that God will vindicate the martyr or pious person who has not received his 'just deserts' in this life. (Note, however, that Isaiah 26:19 may refer to the resurrection of the whole nation.)

By New Testament times, belief in resurrection and judgement was more widely held, at least by the religious party of the Pharisees and by the Essene sect (the community of the Dead Sea Scrolls). It was, however, rejected by the more traditional Sadducees who accepted only the written Law (see Mark 12:18–27). Paul was himself a Pharisee, converted to the Christian 'Way' by an encounter with the risen Christ on the road to Damascus. The resurrection of Jesus was interpreted by the early Christians as the breaking through into the present of an event (the resurrection of *all*) that had been expected in the future, at the end of time. Christ had been raised, Paul claims, as the 'first fruits' or guarantee that believers will also be raised (1 Corinthians 15:20, 23), with an immortal, 'spiritual body' (15:44).

Grounds for hope: arguments

EXERCISE

From time to time people have developed more philosophical arguments in favour of life after death, independently of revelation. Try to list any that you have encountered in reading or conversation.

You might have come across some of the following:
• Some have argued that we each have a non-material soul which is therefore not subject to illness, decay or death, unlike the body. For Plato, the soul is 'simple' (not made up of parts) and therefore imperishable. In our everyday language, 'I' am more than my body and its behaviour. We think that we 'have' bodies but that we 'are' minds or souls. Our bodies are located in space; they are public. Death is something that happens to the body – you can *see* it dying. But 'where' are our minds, our ideas, our thoughts, our creativity, our intentionality? And what evidence is there that *they* die?
• Descartes argued that the only proposition of which I can be certain is that I exist: 'I think, therefore I am.' Thinking, he argued, is unrelated

to the body and the mind can therefore continue without a body. More generally, we cannot doubt that we exist but we can doubt that we have a body (we can conceive ourselves as being without a body).

- Immanuel Kant argued that our sense of duty urges us to develop a perfect will. As this is not achievable in this life we must postulate a life beyond the grave. He also argued that virtue ought to be rewarded by happiness and that God can only ensure this in another world.

- In reaction against the assumption that talk about our souls or minds can be replaced by talk about our brains, Swinburne imagines separating the two hemispheres of the brain of person A and transplanting them into two other bodies (having conveniently emptied their own skulls first). He argues that even if these two 'new' people survive, we will not know what has happened to person A, although we know precisely where his brain is. 'Persons are not the same as their bodies', he writes (Swinburne, 1986, p. 150).

- Parapsychology ('psychical research') suggests that some people can sometimes communicate and experience without using their bodies: through telepathy, psychokinesis, 'out of body' (including 'near-death') experiences, etc.

Of course the sceptic can raise serious criticisms and opposing arguments against each of these claims. You may wish to take a little time to think about your own criticisms of them.

Contrasting views of human nature

For the biblical writers a human being is a unity. Humans are created from the earth and animated by God's Spirit or breath (Hebrew *ruach*, Greek *pneuma*). But there is little hint in Scripture of any dualism of a physical body and a non-material mind or soul capable of independent existence. This 'psychophysical unity' of human nature may be expressed by describing women and men either as 'embodied souls' or as 'ensouled bodies'.

The key question in the Bible is a moral and religious question about whether you (the whole of you) are:
- open in obedience to God as Spirit (whether you are 'spiritual'); or
- self-centred, corrupt and oriented away from God, following only 'natural' passions or desires (whether you are 'fleshly', 'carnal' or 'worldly': see 2 Corinthians 10:2; Galatians 5:16–25).

The standard question about human nature in Greek thinking is very different. It is also a moral and religious question, but it includes a philosophical concern with our true nature and whether it is radically different from, and therefore can escape, this prison of the body and the world. Plato's account of human nature stressed the superiority of the soul (which he regarded as the real person), and its intellectual and contemplative life, over the mortal, changing and insubstantial life of the body, matter and the world of Nature. This *dualistic* view of body and soul has also been very influential in Christian thinking.

Christian conceptions of life after death

EXERCISE
📖 Read 1 Corinthians 15 and Wisdom of Solomon 2:23 to 3:9 (in the Apocrypha).

Briefly note down the main features of these accounts of a life beyond the grave.

Resurrected bodies

The Apostles' Creed of the western (Roman Catholic and Protestant) Churches confesses a belief in the 'resurrection of the flesh', but eastern Christianity speaks more correctly of the 'resurrection of the dead' or the 'resurrection of the body' (Greek *soma*, meaning the whole person: mind and body together). The doctrine has the clearest biblical basis and is a development from the original belief of the Pharisees in a resurrected life after death closely resembling our life before death and expected to take place on earth. Some welcome the emphasis on *bodily identity* in this understanding of life after death, arguing that to be the same person involves having a body 'identical to' or 'continuous with' our earthly body. Others applaud the fact that this doctrine accords with our sense of the importance of having a body of some sort in order to act, communicate and enjoy experiences.

Christians often present the resurrection of Jesus as the paradigm of resurrection, although the New Testament accounts seem to indicate that Jesus' resurrection/body was intermediate between a material body on earth and a 'spiritual body' in heaven, whereas *our* resurrection is to be entirely in heaven (see 1 Corinthians 15:35–57; Philippians 1:19–26; Revelation 20:11 to 21:4). However, liberal theologians sometimes describe Jesus' resurrection as the re-creation or survival of his soul (mind or true self) in heaven, which then manifested his presence to the disciples through a telepathic communication to their minds that gave rise to an 'appearance' of his body (see Badham, 1976, chapter 2). On this view the resurrection appearances were 'veridical hallucinations': hallucinations in that no physical body of Jesus was actually present on earth, but veridical (truthful) in that it was Jesus himself, alive in heaven, who caused these images in the minds of the disciples.

The 'replica theory'. John Hick offers the following analysis of the resurrected afterlife to persuade us of its plausibility. Imagine, he writes, that a person dies and his body and brain (and therefore mind) disintegrate, but are then recreated in heaven. This 'replica' is exactly identical in every respect to the person who has died, consisting of body and mind together but existing in 'another space' (another physical universe, with space-time co-ordinates different from this universe). 'The picture that we have to consider is one in which Mr X dies and his "replica", complete with memory, etc., appears . . . as a resurrection "replica" in a different world altogether, a resurrection world inhabited by resurrected "replicas"' (Hick, 1976, p. 285).

EXERCISE

Imagine that this re-creation happens to you. Hick claims that it would be like waking up from sleep, and that you would not be inclined in either case to doubt your own identity 'as an individual persisting through time'.

Do you agree? What difficulties might be raised by this theory of life after death?

- Is it possible for 'another world' to exist, with its own co-ordinates, which is not related to and does not interact with our physical world?
- If God can recreate one Jeff Astley after his death, God could recreate two identical Jeff Astleys. Which one would be the 'real Jeff Astley'? Perhaps we have to trust God not to indulge himself like this, as it would certainly wreck our ordinary notion of personal identity (see Hick, 1976, pp. 290–295).
- A resurrection world would pose many problems simply because it

contained people *with bodies.* For example, a physical heaven would become overcrowded; resurrected bodies that are replicas of our earthly bodies would be subject to disease and age (and another death?); and if Grandma died when Jimmy was only four years old how could she recognise him when he is resurrected at the age of seventy-five?

Resurrection may seem to be the concept of life after death that is most easily imaginable and makes most sense to us, because it is so like this life. But these criticisms show that the resurrected body and the resurrected world would have to be *very different* from this earthly body and world in order for the concept of resurrection to be coherent (see Badham, 1976, chapters 4 and 5). But if they are so distinct, what is the conceptual advantage of the notion of a life after death with a body?

Immortal souls

This alternative doctrine proclaims the survival of the *disembodied* mind or self after the death of the body. It is prominent in the history of Christian thought, although it appears only as a minority report in the biblical tradition, in the Apocrypha. Traditionally, the two options have been connected by treating the immortal soul as the afterlife state that we enjoy until our bodily resurrection at the 'Last Judgement' (see Chapter 10).

The concept of a disembodied mind has its own problems. How does such a mind perceive, act or communicate? In this world we use physical sense organs, limbs and mouths to fulfil these functions. But in the afterlife described here, we shall have no body at all.

The 'dream world theory'. One answer has been offered by the philosopher Henry Price. He developed an account of a disembodied afterlife that makes it very similar to our present dream experience. It includes the following elements:

- We could have 'post-mortem' (after-death) experiences similar to the perceptions we now enjoy in dreams. They would be mind-dependent and have their 'own space', with one item being at a 'distance' from another. We also 'act' in our dreams by means of a 'dreamed body', for we run along the dream streets as fast as our dream legs will carry us.
- Communication between disembodied minds could take place by telepathy. A telepathic communication from another person might give rise to an appropriate image of that person in the mind of the

recipient. (So perhaps Grandma would see and recognise Jimmy as the infant she knew during her life?)

- Price also argues that people's desires would help fashion the images in their dream worlds:

> If I may put it so, the 'stuff' or 'material' of such a world would come in the end from one's memories, and the 'form' of it from one's desires. To use another analogy, memory would provide the pigments, and desire would paint the picture. One might expect, I think, that desires which had been unsatisfied in one's earthly life would play a specially important part in the process. That may seem an agreeable prospect. But there is another which is less agreeable. Desires which had been *repressed* in one's earthly life, because it was too painful or too disgraceful to admit that one had them, might also play a part, and perhaps an important part, in determining what images one would have in the next. And the same might be true of repressed memories. (Price, 1965, p. 17)

EXERCISE
What are the strengths and the weaknesses of this understanding of the afterlife, in your view?

One problem that particularly stands out is the 'tension between the idea of the formation of a post-mortem world by the power of desire and the idea that such a world is common to many minds in virtue of telepathic links between them' (Hick, 1976, p. 267). Bob Dylan once sang, 'I'll let you be in my dream if I can be in yours' ('Talking World War III Blues'). But if we each determine our own dreams, and I want to play golf all the time while you want to shop continually, how do we even *meet* in the afterlife? A common world seems to be needed for that. It would also be needed for any real relationships or moral progress. If these elements are part of our afterlife, and not all Christians think that they are, God will need to provide us all with the same 'dream' of the same post-mortem world. (Interestingly, the eighteenth-century philosopher George Berkeley suggested that the *present* world was constituted in just this way.)

What criteria of personal identity are satisfied by this account? In the doctrine of immortality there is no continuity of the body after death;

the mind alone, with its memories and character, 'carries on'. Is that enough to make the afterlife dream-you 'the same person' as the present-you?

Perhaps the greatest difficulty is that this proposed afterlife is not a 'real world' at all. You may have responded at first, 'It's just a dream!' But that would be better than nothing and at least heaven would never get overcrowded, for it is only bodies that take up real space.

You may have come up with a wider and more theological objection to belief in immortality. Oscar Cullmann argued that the idea of natural immortality was an alien Greek import into Christianity, by contrast with the genuinely Christian doctrine of a resurrection dependent on God's gracious supernatural activity in a new act of creation (Cullmann, 1958). But a full doctrine of creation, as expounded in Chapter 2, would surely recognise God's free, loving activity in the *continuing* existence of the human soul, even in a disembodied form. Alternatively, it would be possible to reason that a new miraculous act of God is needed to keep the soul in existence, or to recreate it after death.

Reincarnation

This is the idea of the self or soul moving to a new body, often in *this world*, after the death of its first bodily home. Judaism, Christianity and Islam have never adopted this view, except as a minority option (recently by Meynell, 1998, pp. 306–308). It is, however, the standard account of the afterlife in eastern religions and worth considering briefly.

In some forms of Hinduism only our 'subtle body' (*linga sharira*) passes over from one life to the next. This is composed of non-conscious mental elements, such as moral and intellectual dispositions, and includes the 'karmic deposit' resulting from our past good and bad actions. This is similar to the view taken by some Buddhists of our rebirth or 'rebecoming'. On more popular interpretations of reincarnation, however, it is the whole conscious self that migrates from one body to the next.

Some sharp questions about personal identity have been asked of the idea of reincarnation:

• What are the criteria of personal identity between one life and the next if only character dispositions continue between them? Is that enough for us to say that this next person is really 'me'? If a number of people all have 'a Napoleonic character', is that good evidence that they are all reincarnations of Napoleon (or that any one of them is)?

- In some cases, it is said that a person can remember his previous lives. There would then be some continuity of memory, which is our normal subjective evidence in this life for 'being the same person'. But memory is not infallible, and we usually only accept that someone 'remembers' something if we know that he could have been there at the time. But how could Fred be said to remember Joe's past unless Fred's body was present during the events that make up Joe's life?

Who believes what?

According to opinion surveys, belief in the survival of the soul predominates over belief in resurrection of the body, although there are some inconsistent overlaps. In one study of the general British population, 34% affirmed immortality and 18% resurrection, with less than 13% affirming reincarnation. Interestingly, while about a third of the *Anglicans* in this survey expressed a belief in the continuation of the soul after death, only 4% said that they believed in a resurrection. This compares with some 14% affirming reincarnation and a thumping 32% who join Cupitt and others in judging death to be 'the end of life' (Davies, 1997).

So, then, what do *you* believe?

Further reading

Introductory
Astley, J (1995), Thinking about life after death: options and identity, *Dialogue*, 3, 25–29.
Davies, B (1993), *An Introduction to the Philosophy of Religion*, Oxford, Oxford University Press, chapter 11.
Hick, J (1983), *Philosophy of Religion*, Englewood Cliffs, New Jersey, Prentice-Hall, chapters 9 and 10.
Pailin, D A (1986), *Groundwork of Philosophy of Religion*, London, Epworth, chapter 9.
Perry, M (1975), *The Resurrection of Man*, London, Mowbrays.
Peterson, M, Hasker, W, Reichenbach, B, Basinger, D (1991), *Reason and Religious Belief: an introduction to the philosophy of religion*, New York, Oxford University Press, chapter 10.
Vardy, P (1990), *The Puzzle of God*, London, Collins, chapter 18.
Wiles, M (1974), *The Remaking of Christian Doctrine*, Cambridge, Cambridge University Press, appendix pp. 125–146.

Advanced

Avis, P (ed.) (1993), *The Resurrection of Jesus Christ*, London, Darton, Longman and Todd.

Badham, P (1976), *Christian Beliefs about Life After Death*, London, Macmillan.

Badham, P and Badham, L (1984), *Immortality or Extinction?* Basingstoke, Macmillan.

Cohn-Sherbok, D and Lewis, C (eds) (1995), *Beyond Death*, Basingstoke, Macmillan.

Davis, S T (ed.) (1989), *Death and Afterlife*, Basingstoke, Macmillan.

Geach, P (1969), *God and the Soul*, London, Routledge and Kegan Paul, chapters 1 and 2.

Hick, J (1976), *Death and Eternal Life*, London, Collins.

Küng, H (1984), *Eternal Life?* London, Collins.

Ward, K (1985), *The Battle for the Soul*, London, Hodder and Stoughton, chapters 7 and 8.

10.   THE END OF IT ALL?

Introduction

In the previous chapter we took a rather cool and philosophical look at the question of life after death, exploring the logical coherence of different forms of this belief and rehearsing the evidence and arguments that have been used to support it.

But our reflections on death and what might come after it, and about the direction and consummation of God's world, are usually more self-involving, more personal and (in a broad sense) more 'theological' than those of the philosopher. In this chapter we shall seek to address these more existential and Christian concerns about what is involved in 'living towards the End'.

Note that the English word 'end' has more than one meaning. It may refer to a *conclusion*: the farthest point or final part of something, its ultimate condition. Or it may refer to a *purpose*: a thing that one seeks, the 'object for which a thing exists', the 'whole point' of something. In terms of ultimacy and fulfilment of purpose, 'the end is that after which nothing further can happen . . . because there is nothing more to happen' (Robinson, 1968, p. 55). To speak of God or heaven as the end of life, or even to accept that 'death is the end', is to make some claim about the purpose, value and meaning of our lives, in addition to saying what we believe might 'come next'.

Christian theology inherited a theology of hope from the Jewish Scriptures and gave it a new depth and dimension in the light of the resurrection of Jesus and the New Testament teaching about our present and future life 'in Christ'. Nevertheless, Christianity is realistic about death and about how we feel in facing death. Jesus confronts the prospect of his own suffering and death with anguish (Mark 14:32–38; Luke 22:39–45; Hebrews 5:7–8) and Paul represents death as a hostile force – the 'last enemy' to be destroyed (1 Corinthians 15:26).

Reflecting on experience
How do you think and feel about your own life's end? In what ways does Christianity offer you hope, strength or support as you anticipate your death? Is there a more negative dimension to your perspective, as a Christian, on your own death?

The biblical hope

During the last century the Bible was increasingly recognised as an 'eschatological' book. The biblical traditions contain many examples of a people 'looking forward' and 'looking beyond' their present historical and personal predicaments to a new and bolder activity of God in the future.

Israelite faith hoped for a 'day of the Lord', which was interpreted both as deliverance (Isaiah 2:2–4) and as calamity (Amos 5:18–20). In certain strands of Old Testament theology, God's judgement and vindication became connected with human representatives: whether messianic figures ('messiah' simply means 'anointed one') associated with the House of David (as in Isaiah 11:1–9), or symbols of Israel such as the Suffering Servant (Isaiah 52:13 to 53:12) and the suffering-and-vindicated Son of Man (Daniel 7).

The 'apocalyptic' ('revelatory') texts from the Old Testament (the Book of Daniel), the period between the two testaments (for example 1 Enoch, 2 Ezra, 2 Baruch) and the New Testament (Mark 13, the Book of Revelation) shift the focus from human kings and earthly kingdoms to heavenly figures and dramas. They therefore encourage a future hope that looks to a divine fulfilment beyond this world.

These hopes and expectations serve as the backdrop to the drama of Jesus. Jesus confronts people with 'the Kingdom', God's rule.

EXERCISE
📖 Read Matthew 11:1–6; 13:36–42; 16:24–28; Mark 9:1; Luke 9:57–62; 11:20; 17:20–21; Acts 1:6–9.

In the life and words of Jesus, is the Kingdom of God a present reality or a future hope?

The most plausible interpretation is that the Kingdom is already present in Jesus' own ministry and teaching but is yet to come fully 'with power'. Some biblical scholars therefore speak of the Kingdom as 'inaugurated but not yet completed'.

The delay in this completion of God's purposes, and of the 'parousia' or second coming of Christ, profoundly influenced the Christian hope.

EXERCISE

📖 **Read 1 Thessalonians 4:15 to 5:11; Philippians 1:23 and 2 Peter 3:3–13.** (1 Thessalonians is probably the earliest New Testament document and 2 Peter among the last.)

What was likely to be the effect of a deferred or disappointed hope in the second coming of Christ?

You might argue that attention would shift to the ethics and organisation of the Christian life and Church, which could now be recognised as having a future. It is likely too that people would become more concerned about their own end, that is their death, and their own particular 'coming' to face Christ in heaven.

Traditional eschatology

In later Christian piety the eschatological themes are about God's actions beyond this life, indeed beyond the world. More recently, however, an 'earthly eschatology' has been developed that recaptures the this-worldly emphasis of many of the Hebrew prophets, with an emphasis on the political and economic liberation of the oppressed (see Cone, 1970; Gutiérrez, 1988; cf. Moltmann, 1967, pp. 325–338).

But more traditional accounts of 'eschatology', the branch of theology that deals with the 'last things' (Greek *ta eschata*), are concerned with the doctrines of death, judgement, heaven and hell. Eschatology is regarded as a central aspect of the Christian understanding of human nature ('Christian anthropology', which used to be labelled 'the Doctrine of Man'), since it speaks of the end or goal of human life.

Death

Existentialist writers have been concerned to stress that, unlike other types of being, human existence is a 'Being-towards-death' (Martin Heidegger uses the word *Dasein*). Our recognition of the inevitability of our death leads to the distinctively human condition of *angst*: existential anxiety, dread or despair at the apparent lack of meaning in the universe. Accepting our mortality is essential to overcoming this anxiety and existentialist thought insists that this is achieved only as we strive for the personal integrity of authentic existence. This involves living responsibly, accepting our limitations and striving to achieve what we can, while avoiding retreating into impersonal conformity.

Death, it is said, serves as a focus for life, in that our minds concentrate on what is of real and ultimate value to us when things are about to end. The last things may therefore be thought of as the things that are *of ultimate concern*. They are the things about which we must decide now, at what has been called the 'eschatological moment'. Rudolf Bultmann concludes his *History and Eschatology*: 'Always in your present lies the meaning of history, and you cannot see it as a spectator, but only in your responsible decisions. In every moment slumbers the possibility of being the eschatological moment. You must awaken it' (Bultmann, 1957, p. 155).

At least part of what belief in life after death is about is the claim, made by mortal women and men, that they and their decisions *matter*.

EXERCISE

Sample some of the things that have been written about death, by using the index of a good dictionary of quotations or by glancing through any comprehensive anthology of poetry.

Then ask yourself, '*As Christians* should we regret and resist our own death, or welcome and accept it?'

Theology needs to recognise that death is a natural part of the human condition and an essential component of the engine of evolution. It has been suggested that the positive purpose of death is to provide a boundary to make life manageable (as sleep breaks up our worldly life), and to give us a focus through the possibility of finite achievements and growth of character, as well as helping us to see life's meaning as a whole (see Hick, 1973, chapter 13). But an early or a painful death seems more like a curse and that is how the existence of death is treated in the doctrine of the Fall (see Chapter 7). The association of death with sin (Romans 5:12) suggests that it is our alienation from the good purposes of God that sours our attitude to death, along with many other things, making an enemy of that which – in the end – we can *only* accept.

The concluding lines of Dylan Thomas' elegy for his father read:

> Do not go gentle into that good night.
> Rage, rage against the dying of the light.

This is a deep and noble assertion of the value of human life and a valid response to the battle against natural evil (see Chapter 6). But Christian spirituality and human psychology seem to agree that *in the end* rebellion is less fulfilling of a life than acceptance. We may note that acceptance is recognised by many as the last of the 'stages of dying', after the stages of denial, anger, bargaining and depression (Kübler-Ross, 1975).

For Paul, however, it is only 'through our Lord Jesus Christ' that the 'sting of death' is removed and death is 'swallowed up in victory' (1 Corinthians 15:20–28, 51–58; cf. Isaiah 25:8).

Judgement

The traditional scheme of Christian theology combines two moments of God's judgement:

- a personal, individual judgement of the soul at the moment of a person's death; followed by
- a general resurrection and general judgement at the end of all things.

In this way Christian theology also combined the two different beliefs about the nature of the afterlife that we explored in the last chapter: coupling the immortality of the soul with the resurrection of the physical body, reunited with the soul at the Last Judgement. As a consequence, the classic 'flow-chart' of the afterlife looked something like the diagram on p. 108:

The immediate problem with this pattern of things is the nature of the 'intermediate stage' between death and resurrection. If this is regarded as being in time it may be thought of either as a period of 'waiting' or 'sleep', or as a purgatorial or purifying experience in which those who are not worthy to enter into the divine presence at once can continue to develop spiritually. Some who hold to this latter view claim that there may be a 'second chance' of salvation during this period, even for those who have rejected God. (Christ's 'descent into hell' in 1 Peter 3:18–20 suggests this for those who had no chance to encounter Christ during life.) A series of embodied lives or 'mini-reincarnations' in other worlds has even been proposed as a further development of this notion of purgatory (see below).

The practice of offering prayers or masses to assist souls in purgatory is rejected by Protestant churches. Indeed, Protestants frequently argue that any growth or purification in an intermediate state 'would diminish our historic responsibility in this life', preferring a notion of a judgement immediately on death that is 'irrevocable, final and binding' (Schwarz, 1984, p. 573; cf. p. 578). In this way heaven and hell are often 'moved forward' to the date of the particular judgement. The knock-on effect of this is that the idea of a general judgement of all comes to appear even more redundant.

Heaven

Heaven is variously described in Scripture, theology and worship as a banquet, a place of rest, an unending state of worship, a great city, a paradisal garden and a place where we may have a vision of God as he is in himself. We should not, of course, interpret these metaphors any more literally than we would the vivid language that is used about hell.

Questions have been raised about the plausibility of the very notion of heaven, for a number of reasons. I mention two here; you may have others.

- It has been argued that heaven is psychologically inconceivable as a worthwhile continued life because it is too static or repetitious. But our experiences of similar situations in this present life can give us no more than a hint of the quality of such a transcendent state.
- Accounts of the beatific vision (the experience of God as dwelling within the very essence of the soul and thus being perceived from within by direct contact) raise a further difficulty. Can a person who is so closely united with God remain distinct from God? Some theologians have drawn on the writings of Christian mystics as a pointer to a state of intimate union with God that yet preserves our individual existence.

Hell

Many more doubts have been raised about the doctrine of an ever-lasting place of punishment.

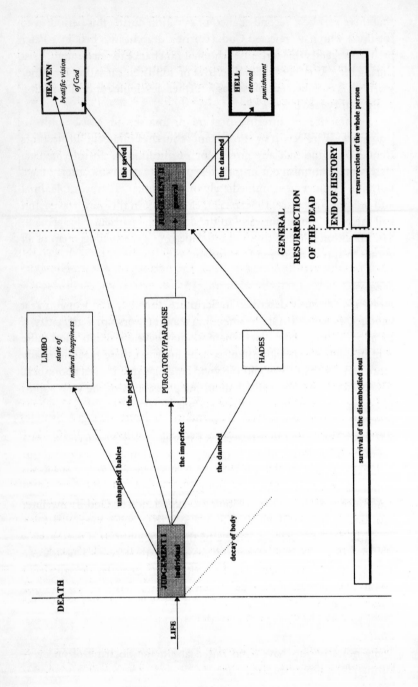

EXERCISE

According to recent opinion polls, 52% of the general population of mainland Britain believe in heaven but only 25% accept that there is a hell. The figures for weekly churchgoers show 89% believing in heaven and 62% in hell (Gill, 1999, pp. 70, 128).

Which category do you fall into? What arguments would you use to defend your view about the existence or non-existence of hell?

New Testament language about hell is also highly metaphorical, in its picturing of a place of despair and separation from God. It sometimes draws on the image of a valley near Jerusalem ('Gehenna' or 'The Valley of Hinnom') where human sacrifice was once offered and where the city's rubbish may have been burned. The impression is one of destruction, or possibly of purification, rather than everlasting punishment – although the 'worms' and 'fire' are said to last for ever (Mark 9:48). 'There is nothing in the traditional doctrines that requires hell to be a place of torture' (Kvanvig, 1997, p. 563) and we should keep in mind that the biblical concept of hell does not regard it as the home of Satan.

We can find affirmations in the New Testament that God's grace and mercy know no bounds (cf. Romans 11:32; 1 Corinthians 15:22; Ephesians 1:10; Philippians 2:9–11). But it cannot be denied that there are also numerous passages that endorse a belief in some form of punishment or loss, most potently perhaps Matthew 25:31–46; Mark 3:29 and Romans 2:6–16.

For many people the 'problem of hell' is the difficulty of morally justifying a purely retributive punishment that lasts for ever. Some argue that punishment can never be justified simply as retribution for wrongs we have done but only if there is some hope of further good consequences, particularly through a process of reformation to create a better person (see another book in this series, Astley, 2000, chapter 7). Further, an *infinite* punishment seems unjust as a response to finite human sin. This is a very different perspective from the claim made by Augustine and others that just punishment is itself part of the proper ordering and beauty of God's creation.

Salvation for all? The assertion that the existence of hell would be fatal to Christian theodicy often rests on the conviction that a God who condemns some to hell will not have brought a good end to every created life. But others doubt whether God *could* ensure the salvation of all without overriding their free will.

Universalism is the belief that all will be saved. It is widely held in liberal theological circles. Despite being rejected in the Church of England's Article 18, it has been recognised as a possible position within the Anglican Church (Archbishops' Commission on Christian Doctrine, 1962, pp. 217–219). Universalism is founded on a firm belief in God's patience, often coupled with Augustine's assertion that God has made us 'for' ('towards') himself (see Chapter 3). Since *our* end (orientation, purpose) is to love God, in *the* end we shall eventually embrace God freely (see Robinson, 1968, p. 133; Hick, 1976, pp. 250–251). Origen and other early theologians held a similar view in the second century but the majority of the theologians of the Church – including Augustine – rejected universalism. It was condemned at the Council of Constantinople in AD 543.

In the last century Karl Barth wrote of 'a truly eternal divine patience and deliverance' that allows us to be open to the possibility of the over-whelming triumph of God's grace in the salvation of all. But we dare not rely on this possibility.

> If we are certainly forbidden to count on this as though we had a claim to it, as though it were not supremely the work of God . . . we are surely commanded the more definitely to hope and pray for it . . . to hope and pray cautiously and yet distinctly that . . . His compassion should not fail, and that in accordance with His mercy which is 'new every morning' He 'will not cast off for ever' (Lamentations 3:22–23, 31). (Barth, 1961, p. 478; cf. 1957, pp. 417–418)

The alternative to universalism is some form of *separationism,* a position that claims to treat our moral religious choices in this life, as well as our freedom and autonomy, more seriously. A moderate form of separationism could allow that *most* humans will in the end be saved, but not all. For many who take a separationist view, and yet believe in a loving God, hell is neither an arbitrary divine punishment, nor 'the conclusive retaliation of a vindictive deity', but merely human 'self-destructive resistance to the eternal love of God' (Migliore, 1991, p. 246). Others argue that the eternally unrepentant will simply cease to exist, a point of view that implies that even though there is no hell, not all will be saved.

Hick is more hopeful. 'Hell exists, but is empty', he writes. 'It is "there" awaiting any who may be finally lost to God; but in the end none are to be finally lost' (Hick, 1973, p. 72). He counsels, however, that hell must still be regarded as a real threat; adding that, in any case, we must all face a 'sort of hell' in the form of a purgatorial experience of 'progressive sanctification after death' – a continuation of the soul-making process which will inevitably involve some suffering (Hick, 1968, p. 383; see above, Chapter 6). The vale of soul-making thus continues in a series of resurrected afterlives (the 'pareschaton') in other resurrection worlds. God may be experienced as more directly present in these worlds, and the pareschaton state will continue until each individual finally fulfils her or his full spiritual and moral potential, transcending selfishness and becoming united with God in the eschaton or 'unitive state' (see Hick, 1976, section V).

Creation and Christ

Many of the topics in this book, including a number in this discussion of 'the End', might be said to fall under the general heading of theism. However, we should not conclude without facing the questions, 'What is distinctive about a *Christian* doctrine of creation (and therefore of providence, suffering, sin, eschatology, and so on)?' and 'What does it mean to speak of this world as the world of a *Christlike* God?'

Some hints towards an answer have already been offered in various places in this book but I shall add here some more explicit reflections.

EXERCISE
📖 Read 1 Corinthians 8:6; Colossians 1:15–20; Hebrews 1:2–3; John 1:1–5.

What do you make of these 'cosmic' claims?

In Jewish thought, God's Wisdom was sometimes seen as the first and fundamental creative act, and even as the agent of creation (cf. Proverbs 8:22–31; Jeremiah 10:12). In the New Testament the highest status ascribed to the figure of Christ is precisely as the agent of creation. For Paul, indeed, it is Christ who is the 'wisdom of God' (1 Corinthians 1:24).

By the fourth century, the most significant title for Christ was the related designation *Logos*. Jesus Christ was God's 'Word', the one who reveals the will and ways of God. But this title also pointed to Christ as 'the Reason and Mind of the cosmos', 'the structure of the universe' (Pelikan, 1985, pp. 62, 65). Because it was created through the Logos, the universe was not to be thought of as absurd or arbitrary; it made sense and it had a proper purpose and goal. And it was this Word, this 'speaking of God', that Christians confessed as having come in the flesh to his world, loving it enough to suffer and die for it. On this view, the reading we make of Jesus is the key to our reading of God and of the world: 'what Jesus did and said points to the underlying meaning and purpose of the creation' (Hefner, 1984, p. 290).

And what is true of the beginning of time is also true at the end. Whatever the end may be for this physical universe of space-time, the Christian hope is for a consummation of all that is of value in it, in and through 'the glorious liberty of the children of God' (see Romans 8:18–23). Some have spoken of this in terms of a formation of the cosmos in the image of Christ to share in the eternal glory, indeed as 'the actualization of the Christ-life in the material structures of being' (Ward, 1998, p. 283). However that may be imagined, for the Christian the last word for the world must somehow relate to the name of Jesus.

So Christ is not only the beginning, the Alpha; he is also the end, the Omega. Whatever is to happen, Jesus remains the goal of the cosmos. In the fullest possible sense, then, God's world – in the end – is Christ's world.

Further reading

Introductory

Farrer, A (1967), *Saving Belief: a discussion of essentials*, London, Hodder and Stoughton, pp. 135–157.

Hebblethwaite, B (1984), *The Christian Hope*, Basingstoke, Marshall, Morgan and Scott.

Lewis, C S (1961), *A Grief Observed*, London, Faber and Faber.

Lewis, C S (1972), *The Great Divide: a dream*, London, Collins.

Macquarrie, J (1978), *Christian Hope*, London, Mowbrays.

McKeating, H (1974), *God and the Future*, London, SCM.

Quick, O C (1963), *Doctrines of the Creed*, London, Collins, chapters XXII–XXIV.

Robinson, J A T (1968), *In the End God*, London, Collins.

Travis, S (1980), *Christian Hope and the Future of Man*, Leicester, Inter-Varsity Press.

Advanced

Anderson, R S (1986), *Theology, Death and Dying*, Oxford, Blackwell.

Barbour, R S (ed.) (1993), *The Kingdom of God and Human Society*, Edinburgh, T and T Clark.

Caird, G B (ed.) (1970), *The Christian Hope*, London, SPCK.

Hick, J (1973), *God and the Universe of Faiths: essays in the philosophy of religion*, London, Macmillan, chapters 5 and 13.

Moltmann, J (1979), *The Future of Creation*, ET London, SCM.

Moltmann, J (1996), *The Coming of God: Christian eschatology*, ET London, SCM.

Paternoster, M (1967), *Thou Art There Also*, London, SPCK.

Pelikan, J (1985), *Jesus through the Centuries: his place in the history of culture*, New York, Harper and Row, chapter 5.

Pittenger, W N (1970), *The 'Last Things' in a Process Perspective*, London, Epworth.

Swinburne, R (1989), *Responsibility and Atonement*, Oxford, Clarendon, chapter 12.

Ward, K (1998), *Religion and Human Nature*, Oxford, Clarendon, chapters 13 and 14.

(See also the further reading for Chapter 9.)

REFERENCES

Allen, D (1990), Natural evil and the love of God, in M M Adams and R M Adams (eds), *The Problem of Evil*, pp. 189–208, Oxford, Oxford University Press.

Alston, W P (1985), God's action in the world, in E McMullin (ed.), *Evolution and Creation*, pp. 197–220, Notre Dame, Indiana, University of Notre Dame Press.

Aquinas (1963–1975), *Summa Theologiae*, ET ed. T Gilby, London, Eyre and Spottiswoode (60 vols).

Archbishops' Commission on Christian Doctrine (1962), *Doctrine in the Church of England (1938 Report)*, London, SPCK.

Astley, J (2000), *Choosing Life? Christianity and moral problems*, London, Darton, Longman and Todd.

Augustine (1961), *Confessions*, ET Harmondsworth, Penguin.

Augustine (1972), *City of God*, ET Harmondsworth, Penguin.

Badham, P (1976), *Christian Beliefs about Life after Death*, London, Macmillan.

Baelz, P (1968), *Prayer and Providence*, London, SCM.

Barbour, I G (1966), *Issues in Science and Religion*, London, SCM.

Barth, K (1957), *Church Dogmatics, Vol. II/ 2*, ET Edinburgh, T and T Clark.

Barth, K (1958), *Church Dogmatics, Vol. III/ 1*, ET Edinburgh, T and T Clark.

Barth, K (1961), *Church Dogmatics, Vol. IV/ 3, I*, ET Edinburgh, T and T Clark.

Brümmer, V (1992), *Speaking of a Personal God*, Cambridge, Cambridge University Press.

Brunner, E (1952), *The Christian Doctrine of Creation and Redemption*, ET London, Lutterworth.

Bultmann, R (1957), *History and Eschatology*, Edinburgh, Edinburgh University Press.

Bultmann, R (1960), *Jesus Christ and Mythology*, ET London, SCM.

Calvin, J (1559), *Institutes of the Christian Religion*, ET various editions.

Clark, M T (ed.) (1972), *An Aquinas Reader*, London, Hodder and Stoughton.

Cobb, J B (1966), *A Christian Natural Theology: based on the thought of Alfred North Whitehead*, London, Lutterworth.

Comstock, G L (1997), Theism and environmental ethics, in P L Quinn and C Taliaferro (eds), *A Companion to Philosophy of Religion*, pp. 505–513, Oxford, Blackwell.

Cone, J H (1970), *A Black Theology of Liberation*, Philadelphia, Lippincot.

Cowburn, J (1979), *Shadows and the Dark*, London, SCM.

Craig, W L (1998), Creation, providence and miracles, in B Davies (ed.), *Philosophy of Religion: a guide to the subject*, pp. 136–162, London, Cassell.

Creel, R E (1997), Immutability and impassibility, in P L Quinn and C Taliaferro (eds), *A Companion to Philosophy of Religion*, pp. 313–319, London, Blackwell.

Cullmann, O (1958), *Immortality of the Soul or Resurrection of the Dead?* ET London, Epworth.

Cupitt, D (1980), *Taking Leave of God*, London, SCM.

Cupitt, D (1992), *The Time Being*, London, SCM.

Darwin, C (1856), Letter to J D Hooker, 13 July 1856.

Davies, B (1993), *An Introduction to the Philosophy of Religion*, Oxford, Oxford University Press.

Davies, D (1997), Contemporary beliefs in life after death, in P C Jupp and T Rogers (eds), *Interpreting Death: Christian theology and pastoral practice*, pp. 130–142, London, Cassell.

Davies, P (1984), *God and the New Physics*, Harmondsworth, Penguin.

Dawkins, R (1988), *The Blind Watchmaker*, Harmondsworth, Penguin.

Dawkins, R (1998), *Unweaving the Rainbow: science, delusion and the appetite for wonder*, London, Penguin.

Dillenberger, J (ed.) (1961), *Martin Luther: selections from his writings*, Garden City, New York, Doubleday.

Doctrine Commission of the General Synod of the Church of England (1991), *We Believe in the Holy Spirit*, London, Church House Publishing.

Edwards, J (1970), *The Great Christian Doctrine of Original Sin Defended*, New Haven, Yale University Press.

Evans, R (1999), *Using the Bible: studying the texts*, London, Darton, Longman and Todd.

Eichrodt, W (1967), *Theology of the Old Testament, Vol. II*, ET London, SCM.

Farmer, H H (1963), *The World and God*, London, Fontana.

Farrer, A (1966), *Love Almighty and Ills Unlimited*, London, Collins.

Farrer, A (1967), *Saving Belief: a discussion of essentials*, London, Hodder and Stoughton.

Flew, A (1955), Divine omnipotence and human freedom, in A Flew and A MacIntyre (eds), *New Essays in Philosophical Theology*, pp. 144–169, London, SCM.

Flew, A (1966), *God and Philosophy*, London, Hutchinson.

Gale, R M (1991), *On the Nature and Existence of God*, Cambridge, Cambridge University Press.

Gaskin, J C A (1984), *The Quest for Eternity*, Penguin, Harmondsworth.

Gilkey, L (1968), Evolution and the doctrine of creation, in I G Barbour (ed.), *Science and Religion*, pp. 159–181, London, SCM.

Gill, R (1999), *Churchgoing and Christian Ethics*, Cambridge, Cambridge University Press.

Gilson, E (1994), *The Christian Philosophy of St Thomas Aquinas*, Notre Dame, Indiana, University of Notre Dame Press.

Griffin, D R (1992), Process theology, in D W Musser and J L Price (eds), *A New Handbook of Christian Theology*, pp. 383–388, Cambridge, Lutterworth.

Gunton, C (1978), *Becoming and Being: the doctrine of God in Charles Hartshorne and Karl Barth*, Oxford, Oxford University Press.

Gunton, C (1997), The doctrine of creation, in C E Gunton (ed.), *The Cambridge Companion to Christian Doctrine*, pp. 141–157, Cambridge, Cambridge University Press.

Gutiérrez, G (1988), *Theology of Liberation: history, politics and salvation*, ET London, SCM.

Habgood, J (1986), Discovering God in action, in T Moss (ed.), *In Search of Christianity*, pp. 108–120, London, Firethorn/Waterstone.

Hartshorne, C (1953), The logic of panentheism, in C Hartshorne and W L Reese (eds), *Philosophers Speak of God*, pp. 499–514, Chicago, University of Chicago Press.

Hartshorne, C (1976), *The Divine Relativity: a social conception of God*, New Haven, Yale University Press.

Hebblethwaite, B L (1979), Some reflections on predestination, providence and divine foreknowledge, *Religious Studies*, 15, 433–448.

Hefner, P J (1984), The creation, in C E Braaten and R W Jenson (eds), *Christian Dogmatics, Vol. I*, pp. 265–357, Philadelphia, Fortress.

Hesse, M (1965), Miracles and the laws of Nature, in C F D Moule (ed.), *Miracles: Cambridge studies in their philosophy and history*, pp. 33–42, London, Mowbray.

Hick, J (1968), *Evil and the God of Love*, London, Collins.

Hick, J (1973), *God and the Universe of Faiths: essays in the philosophy of religion*, London, Macmillan.

Hick, J (1976), *Death and Eternal Life*, London, Collins.

Hick, J H (1981), An Irenaean theodicy, in S T Davis (ed.), *Encountering Evil: live options in theodicy*, pp. 39–52, Edinburgh, T and T Clark.

Hick, J (1983a), *Philosophy of Religion*, Englewood Cliffs, New Jersey, Prentice-Hall.

Hick, J (1983b), *The Second Christianity*, London, SCM.

Hodgson, P C (1994), *Winds of the Spirit*, London, SCM.

Hordern, W (1969a), Creation, in A Richardson (ed.), *A Dictionary of Christian Theology*, pp. 77–79, London, SCM.

Hordern, W (1969b), Man, doctrine of, in A Richardson (ed.), *A Dictionary of Christian Theology*, pp. 202–205, London, SCM.

Hume, D (1902), *Enquiries Concerning the Human Understanding and Concerning the Principles of Morals*, Oxford, Clarendon.

Jacobs, L (1973), *A Jewish Theology*, New York, Behrman House.

Jantzen, G M (1984), *God's World, God's Body*, London, Darton, Longman and Todd.

Jenkins, D (1987), *God, Miracle and the Church of England*, London, SCM.

Keller, E and Keller, M-L (1969), *Miracles in Dispute*, ET London, SCM.

Kitcher, P (1983), *Abusing Science: the case against creationism*, Milton Keynes, Open University Press.

Kübler-Ross, E (1975), *Death, the Final Stage of Growth*, New York, Macmillan.

Kvanvig, J L (1997), Heaven and hell, in P L Quinn and C Taliaferro (eds), *A Companion to Philosophy of Religion*, pp. 562–568, Oxford, Blackwell.

Langford, M (1981), *Providence*, London, SCM.

Lewis, C S (1960), *Miracles*, London, HarperCollins.

Lovelock, J (1988), *The Ages of Gaia: a biography of our living earth*, Oxford, Oxford University Press.

Mackie, J L (1971), Evil and omnipotence, in B Mitchell (ed.), *The Philosophy of Religion*, pp. 92–104, London, Oxford University Press.

Mackie, J L (1982), *The Miracle of Theism: arguments for and against the existence of God*, Oxford, Clarendon.

MacKinnon, D (1968), *Borderlands of Theology*, London, Lutterworth.

Macquarrie, J (1966), *Principles of Christian Theology*, London, SCM.

Mascall, E L (1945), *He Who Is*, London, Longmans, Green.

Mascall, E L (1956), *Christian Theology and Natural Science: some questions on their relations*, London, Longmans, Green.

McFague, S (1993), *The Body of God: an ecological theology*, Minneapolis, Fortress.

Meynell, H (1998), People and life after death, in B Davies (ed.), *Philosophy of Religion: a guide to the subject*, pp. 286–310, London, Cassell.

Migliore, D L (1991), *Faith Seeking Understanding: an introduction to Christian theology*, Grand Rapids, Michigan, Eerdmans.

Moltmann, J (1967), *Theology of Hope*, ET London, SCM.

Moltmann, J (1974), *The Crucified God*, ET London, SCM.

Moltmann, J (1985), *God in Creation: an ecological doctrine of creation*, ET London, SCM.

Moltmann, J (1989), *Creating a Just Future: the politics of peace and the ethics of creation in a threatened world*, London, SCM.

Norris, R A (1966), *God and the World in Early Christian Thought: a study in Justin Martyr, Irenaeus, Tertullian and Origen*, London, A and C Black.

O'Donovan, O (1986), *On the Thirty-Nine Articles: a conversation with Tudor Christianity*, Exeter, Paternoster.

O'Hear, A (1989), *An Introduction to the Philosophy of Science*, Oxford, Clarendon.

Ogden, S (1977), *The Reality of God and Other Essays*, San Francisco, Harper and Row.

Owen, H P (1971), *Concepts of Deity*, London, Macmillan.

Pailin, D A (1989), *God and the Processes of Reality: foundations of a credible theism*, London, Routledge.

Peacocke, A R (1979), *Creation and the World of Science*, Oxford, Clarendon.

Peacocke, A (1993), *Theology for a Scientific Age: being and becoming – natural, divine and human*, London, SCM.

Peacocke, A (1996), *God and Science: a quest for Christian credibility*, London, SCM.

Pelikan, J (1985), *Jesus through the Centuries: his place in the history of culture*, New York, Harper and Row.

Phillips, D Z (1965), *The Concept of Prayer*, London, Routledge and Kegan Paul.

Phillips, D Z (1970), *Death and Immortality*, London, Macmillan.

Pike, N (1970), *God and Timelessness*, London, Routledge and Kegan Paul.

Pittenger, N (1969), *Alfred North Whitehead*, London, Lutterworth.

Polkinghorne, J (1986), *One World: the interaction of science and theology*, London, SPCK.

Polkinghorne, J (1994), *Science and Christian Belief: theological reflections of a bottom-up thinker*, London, SPCK.

Pollard, W G (1958), *Chance and Providence: God's action in a world governed by scientific law*, London, Faber and Faber.

Price, H H (1965), Survival and the idea of 'another world', in J R Smythies (ed.), *Brain and Mind*, pp. 1–33, London, Routledge and Kegan Paul.

Price, H H (1972), *Essays in Philosophy of Religion*, Oxford, Clarendon.

Purtill, R L (1978), *Thinking about Religion*, Englewood Cliffs, New Jersey, Prentice-Hall.

Quinn, P L (1997), Sin and original sin, in P L Quinn and C Taliaferro (eds), *A Companion to Philosophy of Religion*, pp. 541–548, Oxford, Blackwell.

Ringgren, H (1963), *The Faith of the Psalmists*, Philadelphia, Fortress.

Robinson, J A T (1968), *In the End God*, London, Collins.

Rolston, H (1987), *Science and Religion: a critical survey*, New York, Random House.

Schleiermacher, F D E (1958), *On Religion: speeches to its cultured despisers*, ET New York, Harper and Row.

Schwarz, H (1984), Eschatology, in C E Braaten and R W Jenson (eds), *Christian Dogmatics, Vol. II*, pp. 471–587, Philadelphia, Fortress.

Strange, W (2000), *The Authority of the Bible*, London, Darton, Longman and Todd.

Stump, E (1979), Petitionary prayer, *American Philosophical Quarterly*, 16, 81–91.

Suchocki, M H (1992), Panentheism, in D W Musser and J L Price (eds), *A New Handbook of Christian Theology*, pp. 340–343, Cambridge, Lutterworth.

Swinburne, R (1977a), The problem of evil, in S C Brown (ed.), *Reason and Religion*, pp. 81–102, Ithaca, Cornell University Press.

Swinburne, R (1977b), *The Coherence of Theism*, Oxford, Clarendon.

Swinburne, R (1979), *The Existence of God*, Oxford, Clarendon.

Swinburne, R (1986), *The Evolution of the Soul*, Oxford, Clarendon.

Swinburne, R (1994), *The Christian God*, Oxford, Clarendon.

Taylor, R (1963), *Metaphysics*, Englewood Cliffs, New Jersey, Prentice-Hall.

Temple, W (1953), *Nature, Man and God*, London, Macmillan.

Tennant, F R (1906), *The Origin and Propagation of Sin*, Cambridge, Cambridge University Press.

Tillich, P (1968), *Systematic Theology*, Welwyn, Nisbet.

Tracy, T F (1984), *God, Action, and Embodiment*, Grand Rapids, Michigan, Eerdmans.

Vardy, P (1992), *The Puzzle of Evil*, London, HarperCollins.

von Rad, G (1972), *Genesis*, ET London, SCM.

von Rad, G (1975), *Old Testament Theology, Vol. 1*, ET London, SCM.

Ward, K (1982), *Rational Theology and the Creativity of God*, Oxford, Blackwell.

Ward, K (1990), *Divine Action*, London, Collins.

Ward, K (1996a), *God, Chance and Necessity*, Oxford, Oneworld.

Ward, K (1996b), *Religion and Creation*, Oxford, Clarendon.

Ward, K (1998), *Religion and Human Nature*, Oxford, Clarendon.

Westermann, C (1971), *Creation*, ET London, SPCK.

White, L (1967), The historical roots of our ecological crisis, *Science*, 155 (3767), 1203–1207.

Whitehead, A N (1926), *Religion in the Making*, Cambridge, Cambridge University Press.

Whitehead, A N (1967), *Process and Reality: an essay in cosmology*, New York, Macmillan.

Wiles, M (1986), *God's Action in the World*, London, SCM.

Williams, N P (1927), *The Ideas of the Fall and of Original Sin*, London, Longmans, Green.

ET indicates 'English translation'

GLOSSARY AND BIOGRAPHY

agnostic not knowing (particularly whether God exists)

angst existential anxiety in the face of the human condition

apocalyptic revelations, particularly of present and future heavenly events and their effects on this world

apologetics the intellectual defence of belief

Aquinas, St Thomas (1225–1274) philosopher and theologian

Aristotle (384–322 BC) Greek philosopher

Augustine, St (354–430) Bishop of Hippo in North Africa

autonomy the state of being independent and 'self governed' (as opposed to **heteronomy**)

Barth, Karl (1886–1968) Swiss Protestant theologian

basic action an action performed directly, not by doing anything else: for example a human raising an arm or God creating, sustaining or intervening in Nature

beatific vision direct unmediated vision of God as he is in himself

Berkeley, George (1685–1753) Irish philosopher

Brunner, H Emil (1889–1966) Swiss Protestant theologian

Bultmann, Rudolf (1884–1976) German New Testament scholar and radical existentialist theologian

Calvin, John (1509–1564) French Protestant Reformer

continuing creation God's preservation of the universe in being

covenant an agreement, particularly with God

Cranmer, Thomas (1489–1556) English Protestant Reformer and archbishop

creationists those who oppose the theory of evolution and treat the Genesis accounts of creation as scientifically accurate

Darwin, Charles (1809–1882) English scientist

deism the belief that God once brought the universe into existence but has no continuing contact with it

Descartes, René (1598–1650) French philosopher

determinism the view that every event in the universe, including every human action, is wholly and inevitably caused ('determined') by previous events

discarnate/disembodied without a body

dualism any view that divides reality, or some part of reality, into two principles or elements: for example two gods; mind and body

Edwards, Jonathan (1703–1758) American Protestant theologian

empirical given through sense experience

Enlightenment, the eighteenth-century 'Age of Reason', advocated 'trusting your own reason' and critical of reliance on authority and tradition

eschatology beliefs about 'the end of history', 'the future hope' and the 'last things' (death, judgement, heaven and hell)

existentialism a philosophy that emphasises individual choice and resists rational cosmic explanations

Farrer, Austin M (1904–1968) Anglican philosophical theologian

Gnosticism a religious philosophy that disparaged matter and this life, and sought escape for the soul through secret knowledge

Heidegger, Martin (1889–1976) German existentialist philosopher

Heraclitus (died after 480 BC) Greek philosopher

heresy a belief considered as not **orthodox** (the 'right opinion') by the Church

Hume, David (1711–1776) Scottish Enlightenment philosopher

immanent closely involved with, indwelling

immutable unchanging

impassible not subject to suffering, feeling no emotion

incarnation 'enfleshing' (of God in Christ)

indeterminate an event not wholly determined by previous events

Irenaeus, St (c. 115–190) Bishop of Lyons

Kant, Immanuel (1724–1804) German Enlightenment philosopher

Kierkegaard, Søren A (1813–1855) Danish philosopher

Kingdom of God/Heaven God's reign

Leibniz, Gottfried W (1646–1716) German philosopher

Luther, Martin (1483–1546) German Protestant Reformer

materialism the conviction that only matter exists

metaphysics general claims about reality as a whole, often going beyond sense experience

naturalism the belief that reality is understandable without reference to supernatural events or beings

non-realism (in theology) the belief that God is a concept and ideal rather than a reality

numinous a daunting but alluring experience of awe and mystery

omnipotence the ability to do anything that can be done

omniscience the ability to know anything that can be known

ontology the study of being

Origen (c. 185–254) theologian from Alexandria

panentheism the belief that the universe exists within God

pantheism the belief that God is identical to the universe

parousia the second coming of Christ to judge the world

Pelagius (died c. 410) British theologian

penance/reconciliation the act and ritual of making confession for sin

personal identity being the same person over a period of time

Plato (c. 429–347 BC) Greek philosopher

predestination/foreordination the doctrine that events are fixed in advance by God, including our salvation or damnation

prehension (in process thought) the 'feeling' or perception possessed by all events

purgatory temporary place or period of purification through suffering ('purgation')

relativism the view that truth is relative to people, not absolute and objective

sacrament an object or human act that expresses and conveys God's grace

Schleiermacher, Friedrich D E (1768–1834) German Liberal Protestant theologian

separationism the belief that not all people will be saved

soft determinism the claim that freedom of the will is merely freedom from external constraints

Spinoza, Benedict de (1632–1677) Dutch Jewish philosopher

Temple, William (1881–1944) Anglican theologian and archbishop

Tennant, F R (1866–1957) Anglican philosophical theologian

theism the belief that God creates a separate universe and continues to keep it in existence

Thirty-Nine Articles sixteenth-century formulae that attempt to define the doctrine of the Church of England

transcendent that which excels or surpasses; what is beyond and above experience, language, knowledge and thought

universalism the belief that all people will be saved in the end

voluntarism a position that stresses the will; sometimes used of the belief that God directly causes every event in the world, instead of working through the medium of natural causes

Whitehead, Alfred North (1861–1947) English-American philosopher

INDEX OF THEMES

Applying for the Church Colleges' Certificate Programme

The certificate programme is available in Anglican Church Colleges of Higher Education throughout England and Wales. There are currently hundreds of students on this programme, many with no previous experience of study of this kind. There are no entry requirements. Some people choose to take Certificate courses for their own interest and personal growth, others take these courses as part of their training for ministry in the church. Some go on to complete the optional assignments and, after the successful completion of three courses, gain the Certificate. Courses available through the *Exploring Faith: theology for life* series are ideal for establishing ability and potential for studying theology and biblical studies at degree level, and they provide credit onto degree programmes.

For further details of the Church Colleges' Certificate programme, related to this series, please contact the person responsible for Adult Education in your local diocese or one of the colleges at the addresses provided:

The Administrator of Part-time Programmes, Department of Theology and Religious Studies, Chester College, Parkgate Road, CHESTER, CH1 4BJ ☎ 01244 375444

The Registry, Roehampton Institute, Froebel College, Roehampton Lane, LONDON, SW15 5PJ ☎ 020 8392 3087

The Registry, Canterbury Christ Church University College, North Holmes Road, CANTERBURY, CT1 1QU ☎ 01227 767700

The Registry, College of St Mark and St John, Derriford Road, PLYMOUTH, PL6 8BH ☎ 01752 636892

The Registry, Trinity College, CARMARTHEN, Carmarthenshire, SA31 3EP ☎ 01267 676767

Church Colleges' Programme, The Registry, King Alfred's College, Sparkford Road, WINCHESTER, SO22 4NR ☎ 01962 841515

Part-time Programmes, The Registry, College of St Martin, Bowerham Road, LANCASTER, LA1 3JD ☎ 01524 384529